**EASY PIANO**

# KATY PERRY

# PRISM

ISBN 978-1-4803-6862-0

**HAL•LEONARD®**
CORPORATION

7777 W. BLUEMOUND RD. P.O. BOX 13819 MILWAUKEE, WI 53213

In Australia Contact:
**Hal Leonard Australia Pty. Ltd.**
4 Lentara Court
Cheltenham, Victoria, 3192 Australia
Email: ausadmin@halleonard.com.au

Visit Hal Leonard Online at
**www.halleonard.com**

# ROAR

Words and Music by KATY PERRY,
LUKASZ GOTTWALD, MAX MARTIN,
BONNIE McKEE and HENRY WALTER

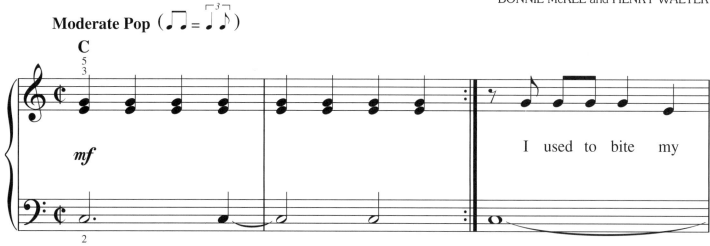

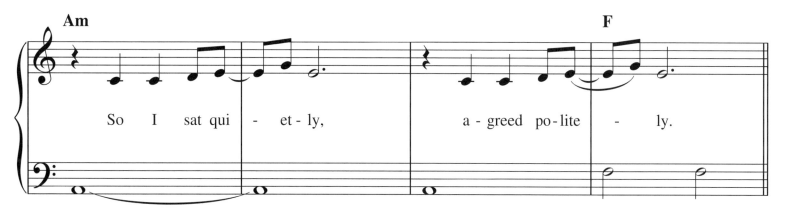

I guess that I for - got I had __ a choice.
Now I'm float - in' like a but - ter - fly.

I let you push me
Sting - in' like a

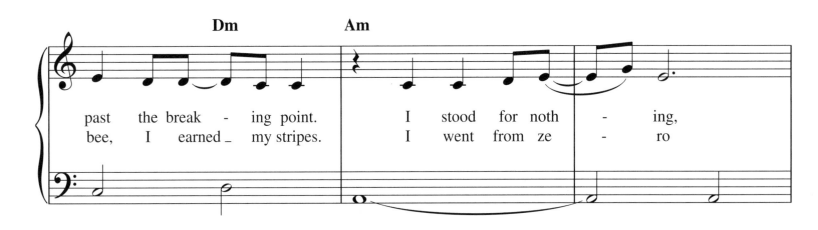

past the break - ing point.
bee, I earned __ my stripes.

I stood for noth - ing,
I went from ze - ro

so I fell for ev - 'ry - thing.
to my own he - ro.

You held me down, but

I got up.

Al - read - y brush - ing off the dust. You

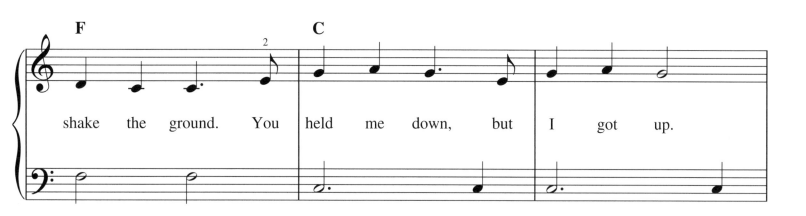

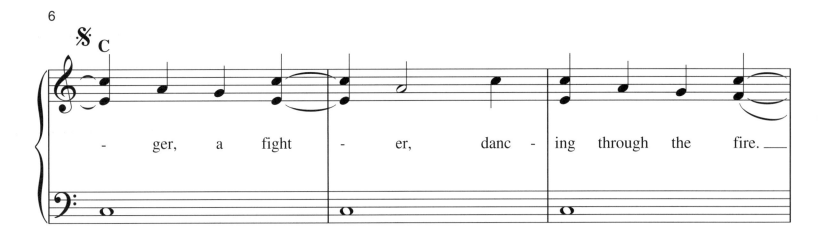

- ger, a fight - er, danc - ing through the fire. ___

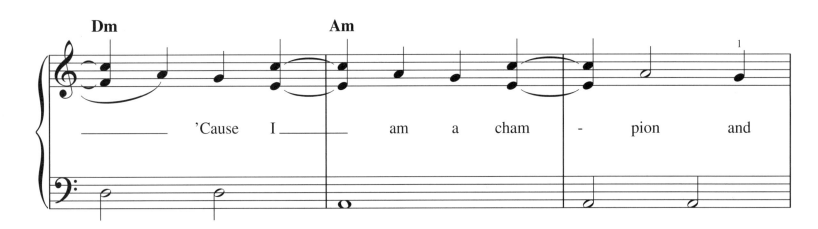

_____ 'Cause I ___ am a cham - pion and

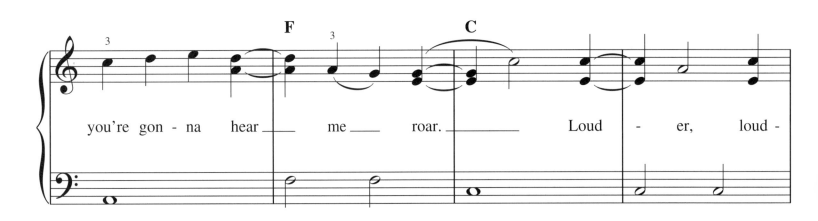

you're gon - na hear ___ me ___ roar. _____ Loud - er, loud -

er than a li - on 'cause I ___ am a cham -

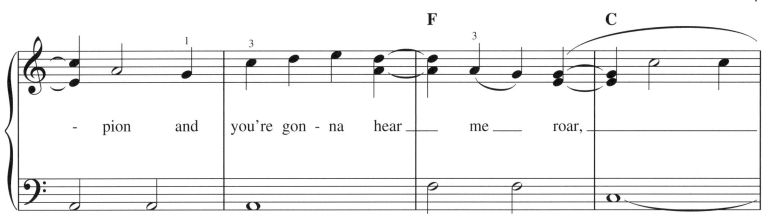

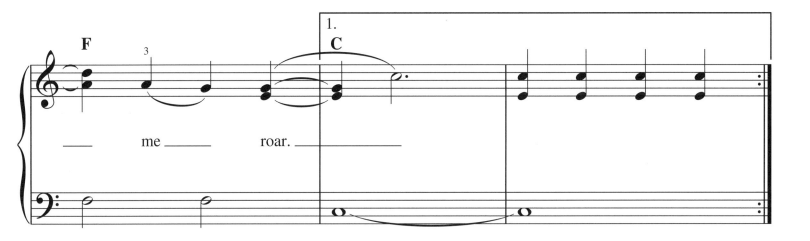

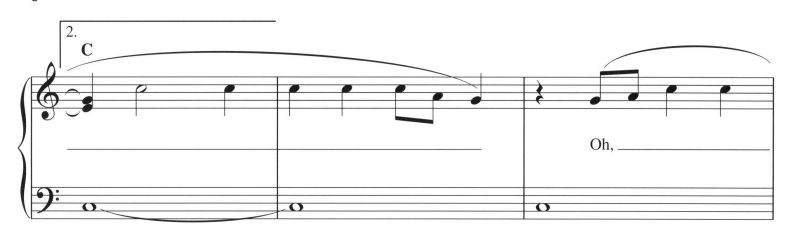

Oh,

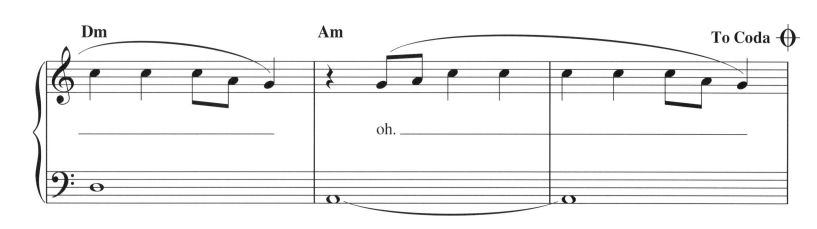

oh.

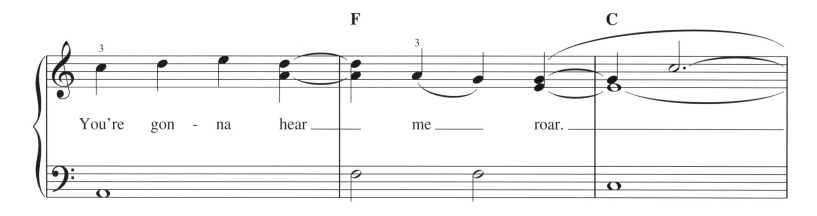

You're gon - na hear me roar.

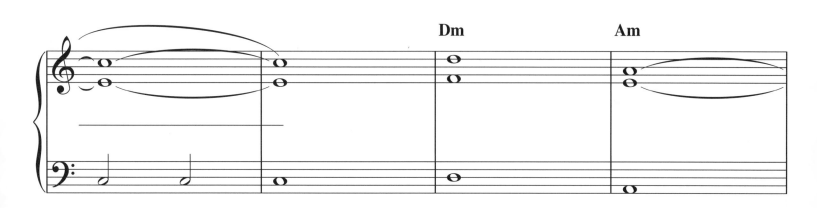

**G**

Roar, _____ oh, _____ roar, _____

oh, _____ roar. _____

**D.S. al Coda**
**(take 2nd ending)**

**CODA**

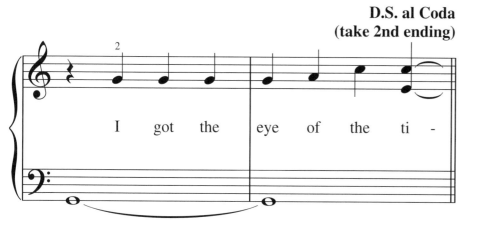

I got the eye of the ti -

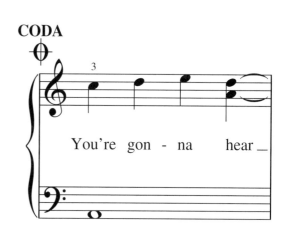

You're gon - na hear _

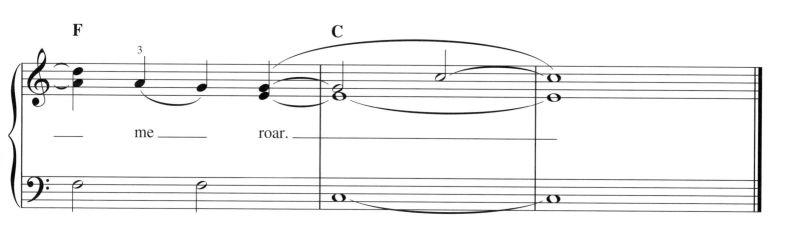

**F**

_ me _____ roar. _____

**C**

# LEGENDARY LOVERS

Words and Music by KATY PERRY,
LUKASZ GOTTWALD, MAX MARTIN,
BONNIE McKEE and HENRY WALTER

**Em** ... **D**

You are my des - ti - ny, my man - tra. I ___
an - y - thing for your love, a ride or die. ___

**C** ... **G**

___ nev - er knew I could see some - thing so clear - ly, look - ing through my third

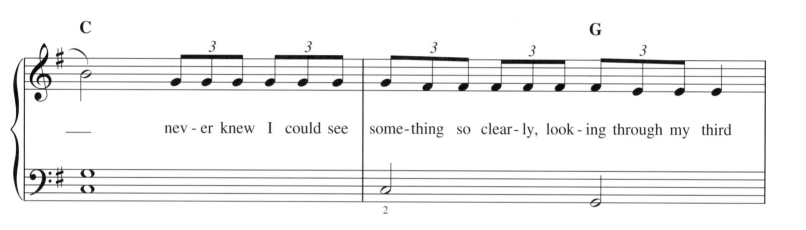

**Em** ... **D**

eye, nev - er knew kar - ma could be so re - ward - ing and bring me to your

**C** ... **G**

light. May - be this is the be - gin - ning of some - thing so mag - i - cal to -

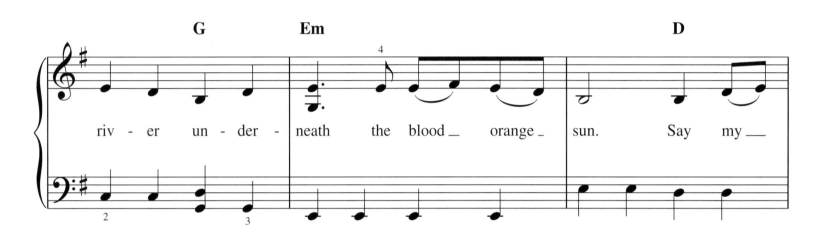

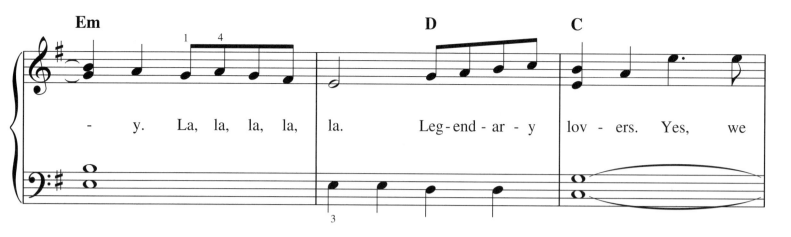

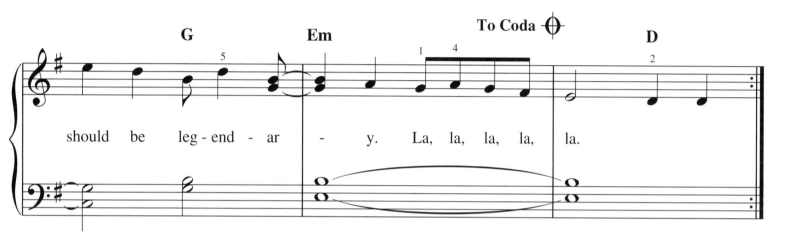

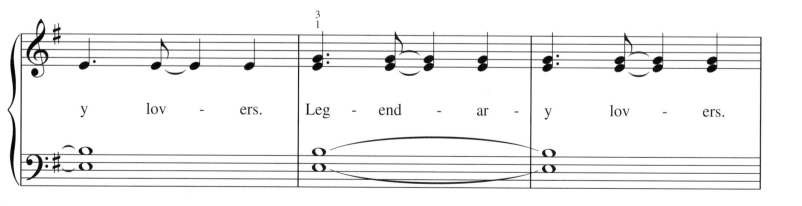

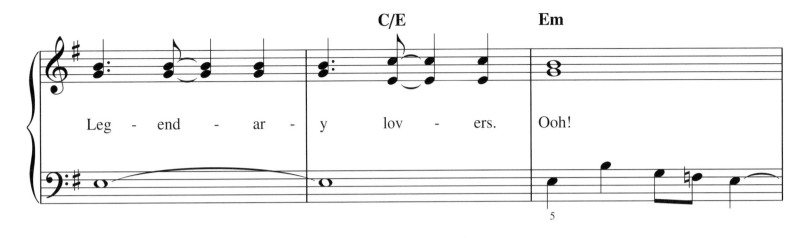

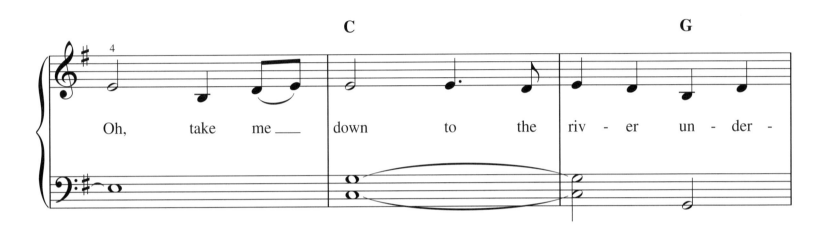

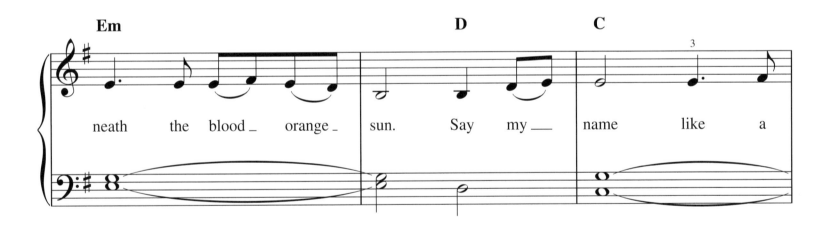

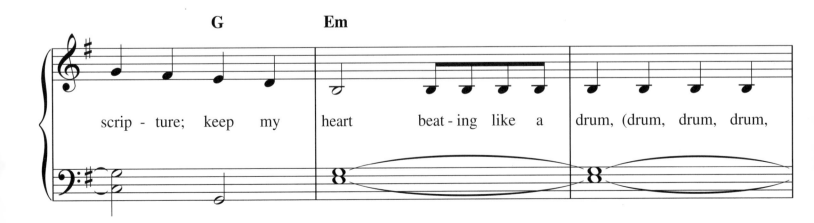

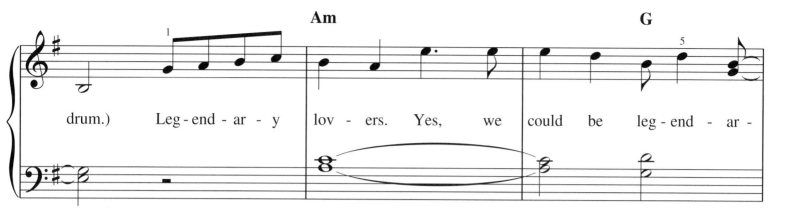

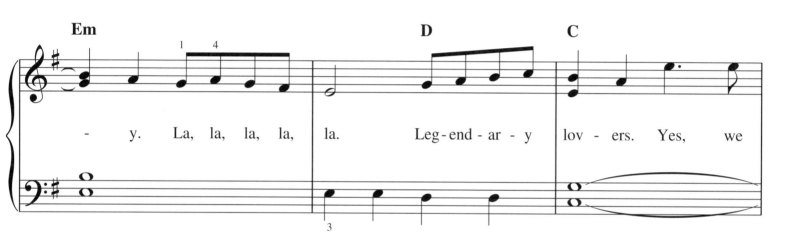

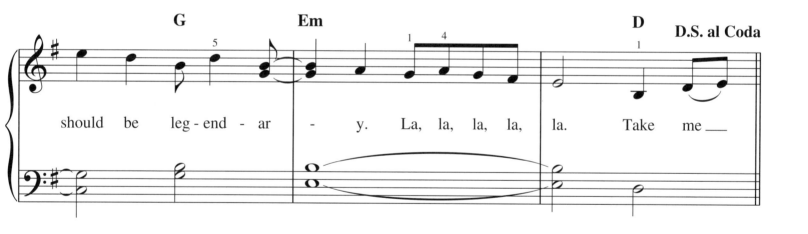

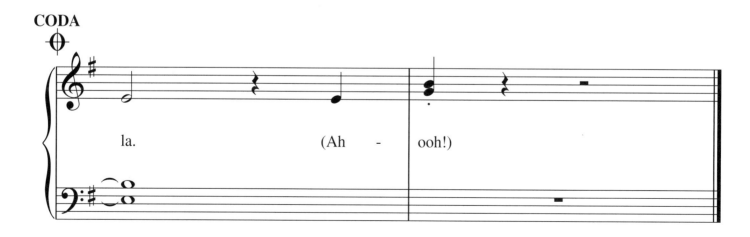

# BIRTHDAY

Words and Music by KATY PERRY,
LUKASZ GOTTWALD, MAX MARTIN,
BONNIE McKEE and HENRY WALTER

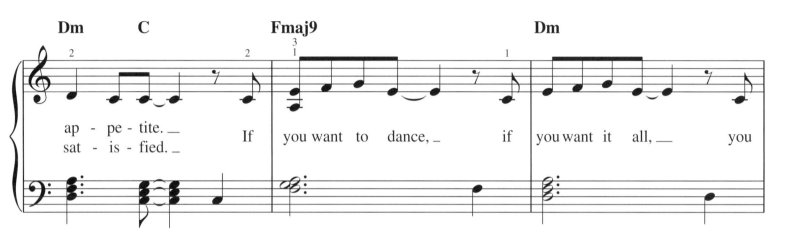

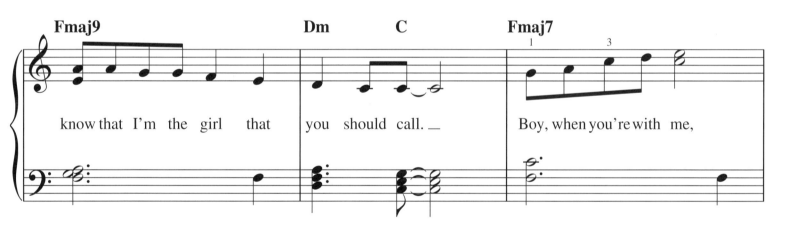

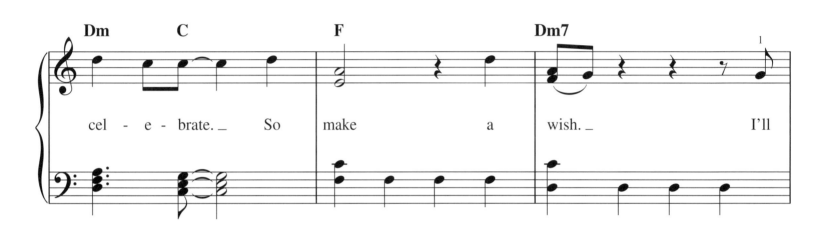

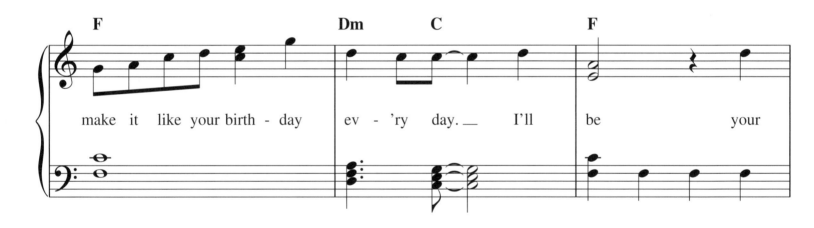

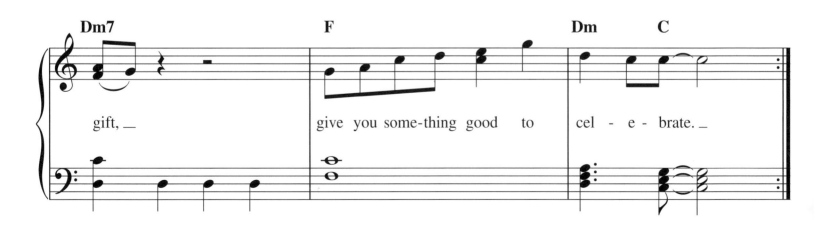

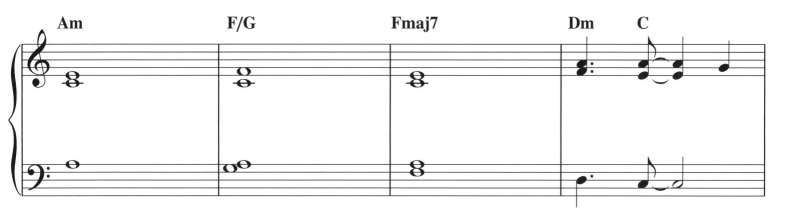

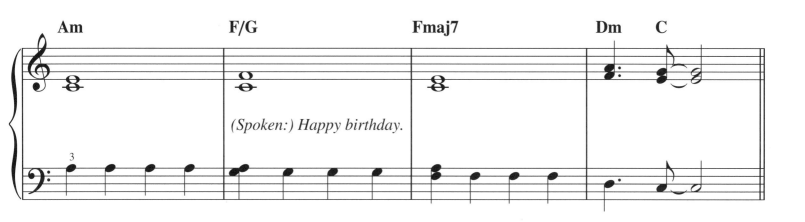

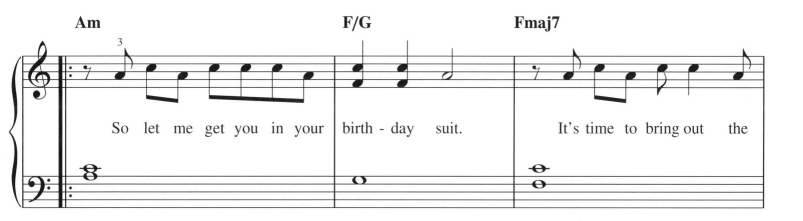

*(Spoken:) Happy birthday.*

So let me get you in your birth - day suit. It's time to bring out the

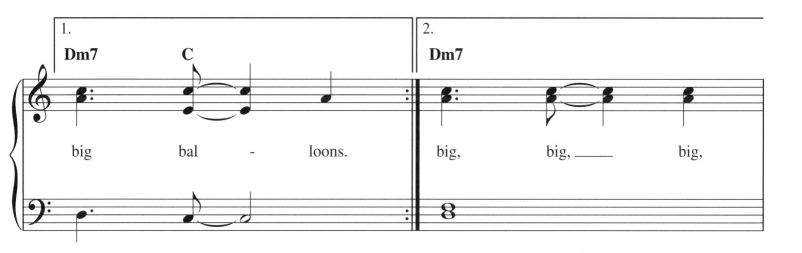

big bal - loons. big, big, _____ big,

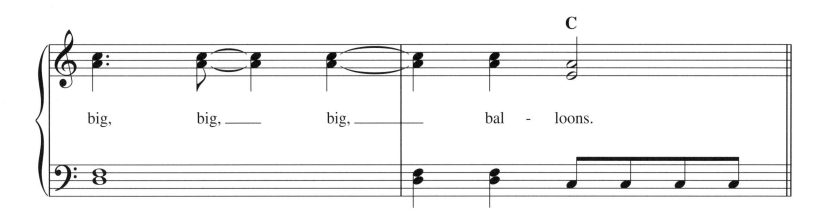

big,        big, _____        big, _____            bal - loons.

**Fmaj7**                    **Dm7**                    **F**

Boy, when you're with me,        I'll give you  a taste,        make it  like your birth - day

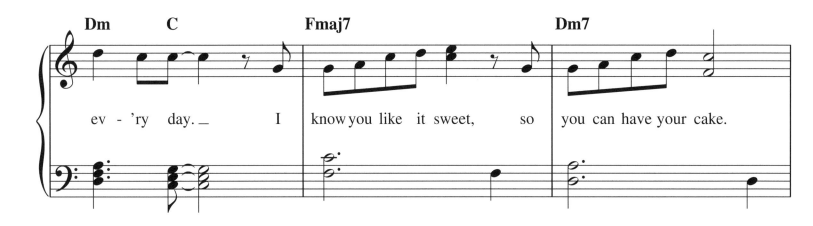

**Dm**        **C**            **Fmaj7**                    **Dm7**

ev - 'ry day. _        I        know you like  it sweet,        so        you can have your cake.

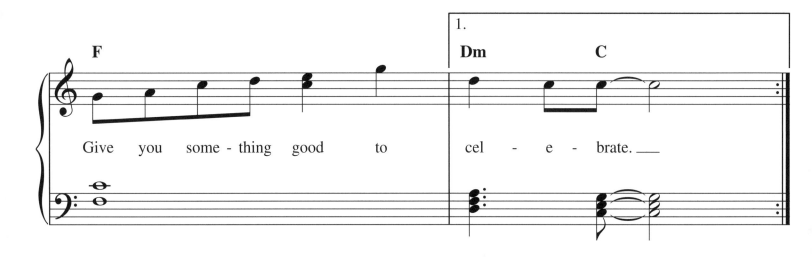

**F**                                        1.
                                            **Dm**        **C**

Give  you  some - thing  good  to        cel  -  e - brate. _____

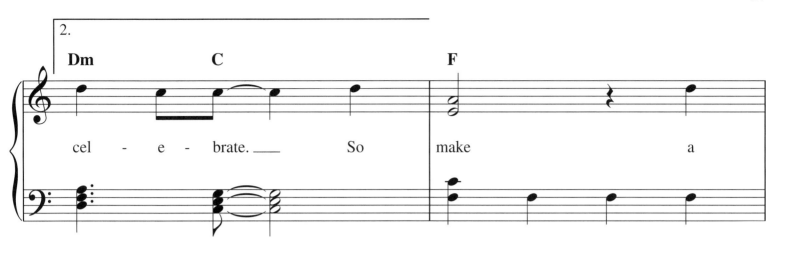

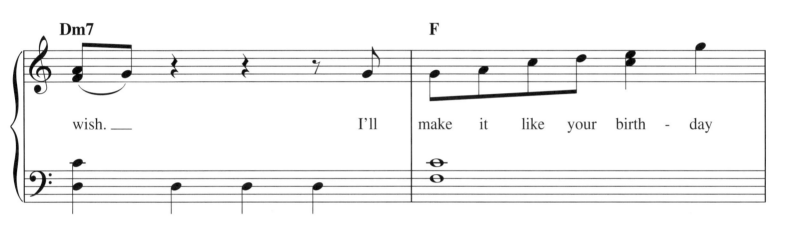

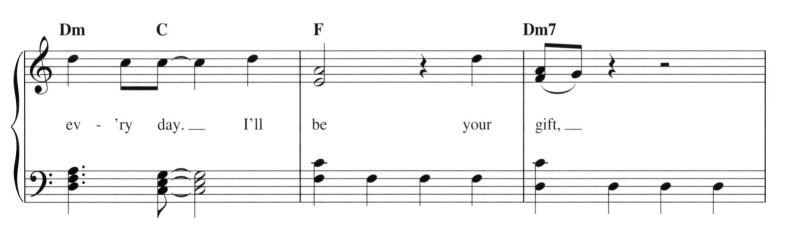

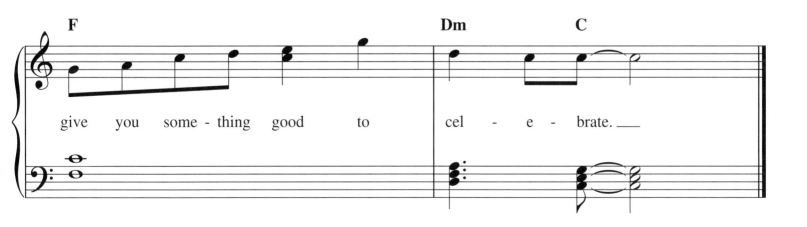

# WALKING ON AIR

Words and Music by KATY PERRY,
KLAS AHLUND, MAX MARTIN,
ADAM BAPTISTE and CAMELA LEIERTH

**Moderate Dance groove**

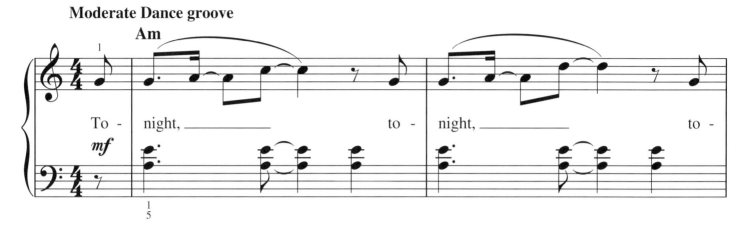

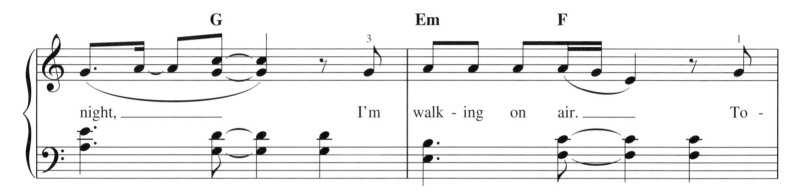

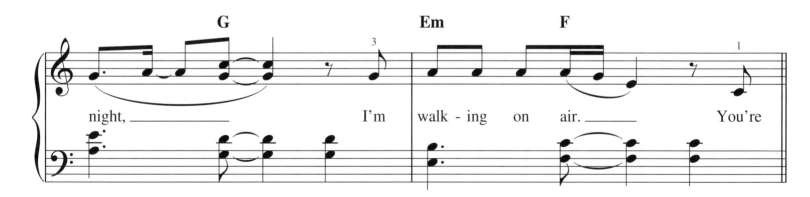

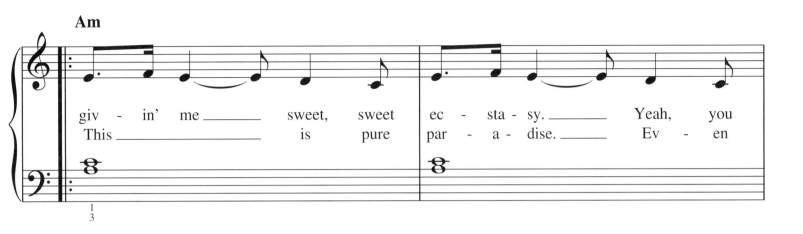

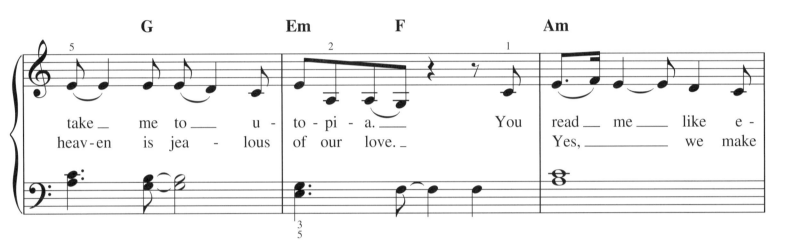

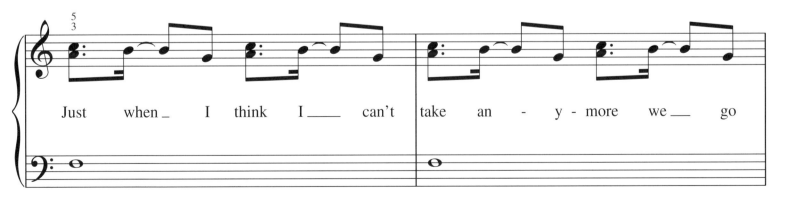

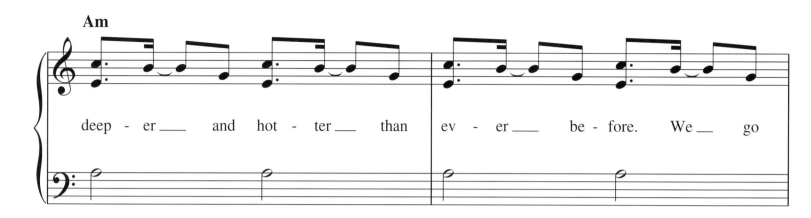

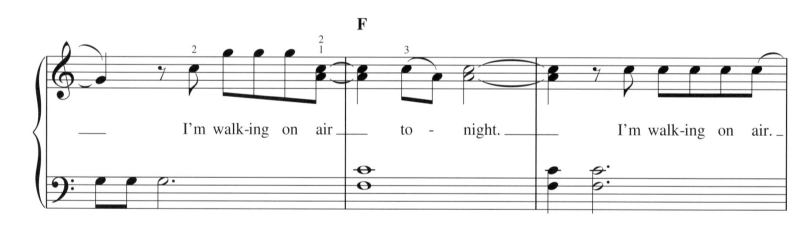

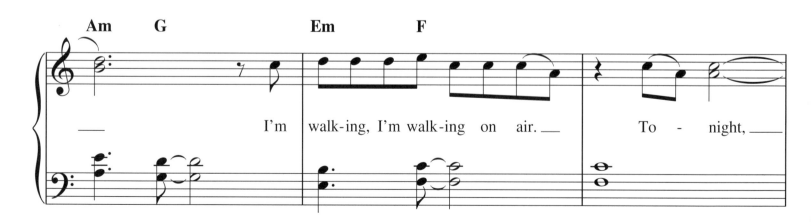

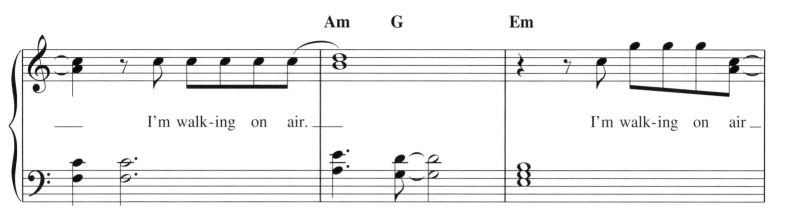

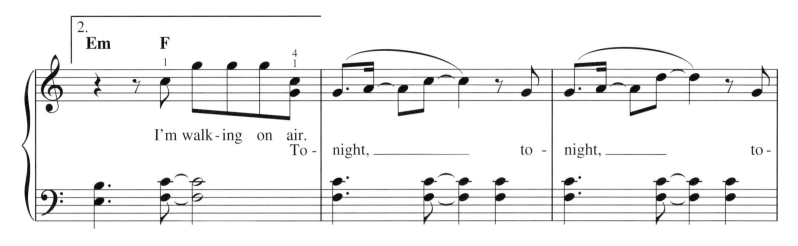

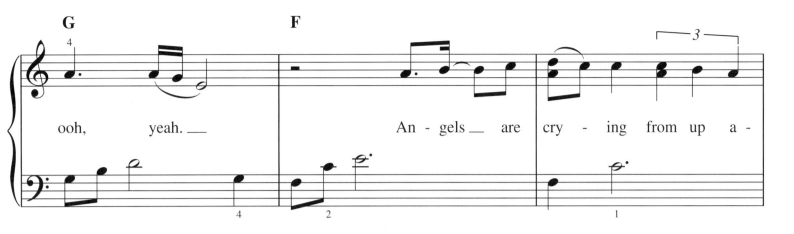

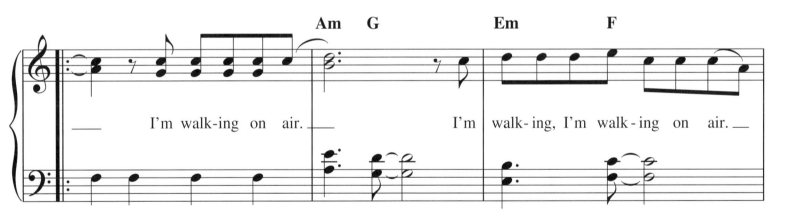

# UNCONDITIONALLY

Words and Music by KATY PERRY,
LUKASZ GOTTWALD, MAX MARTIN
and HENRY WALTER

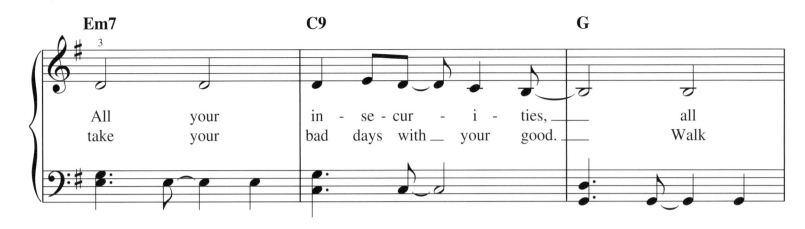

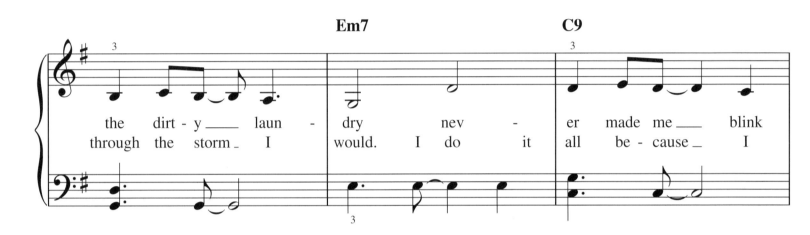

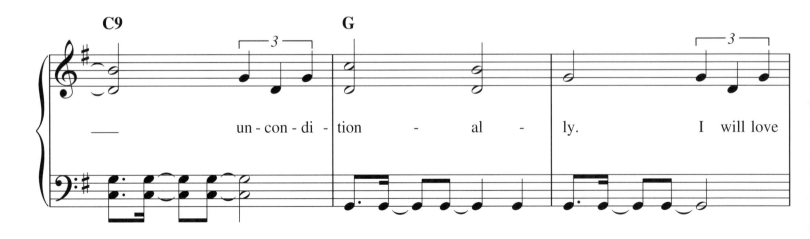

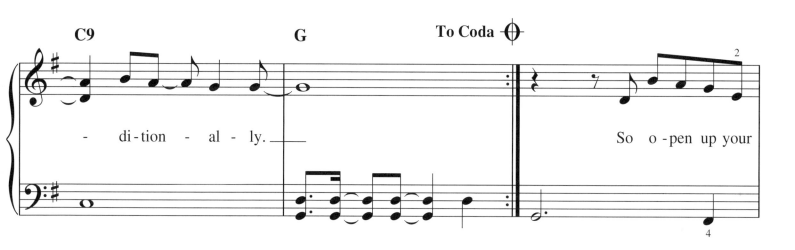

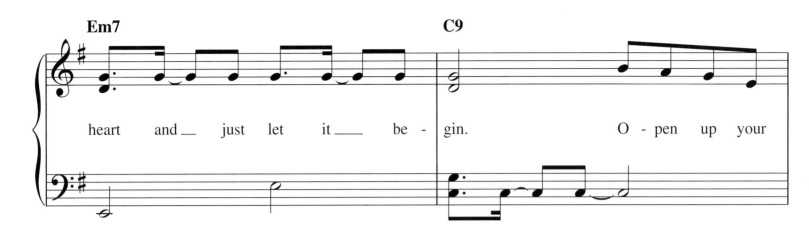

heart and __ just let it __ be - gin.          O - pen up your

heart and __ just let it __ be - gin.          O - pen up your

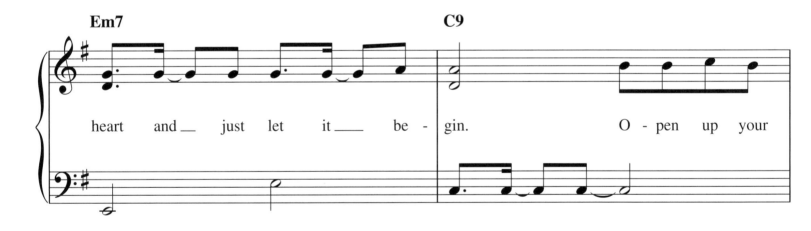

heart and __ just let it __ be - gin.          O - pen up your

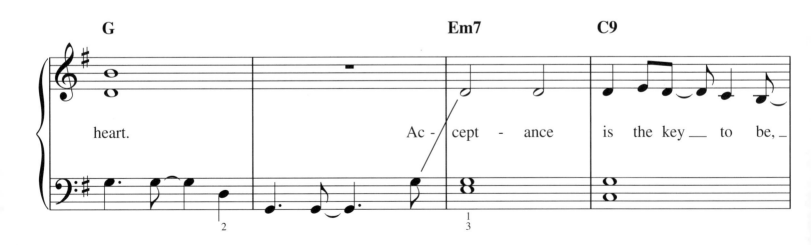

heart.          Ac - / cept - ance     is the key __ to be, __

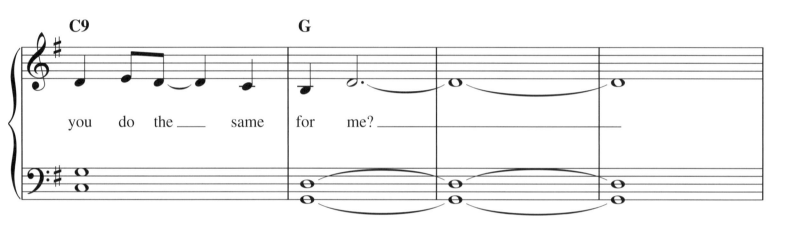

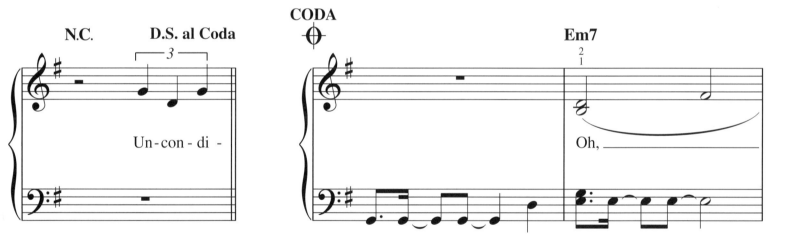

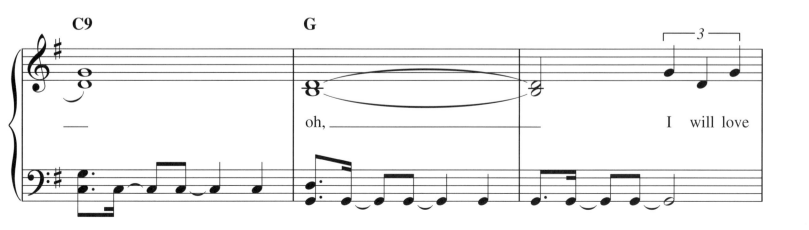

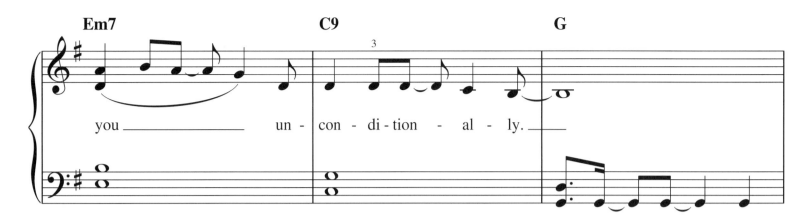

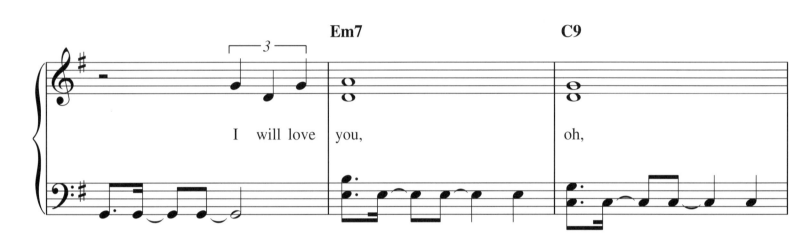

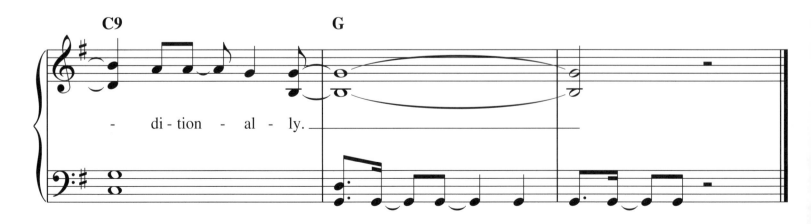

# DARK HORSE

Words and Music by KATY PERRY,
JORDAN HOUSTON, LUKASZ GOTTWALD,
SARAH HUDSON, MAX MARTIN
and HENRY WALTER

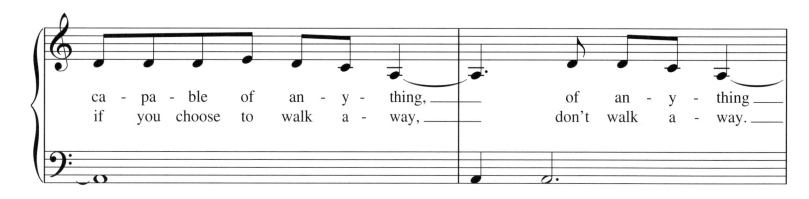

ca - pa - ble of an - y - thing, _____ of an - y - thing _____
if you choose to walk a - way, _____ don't walk a - way. _____

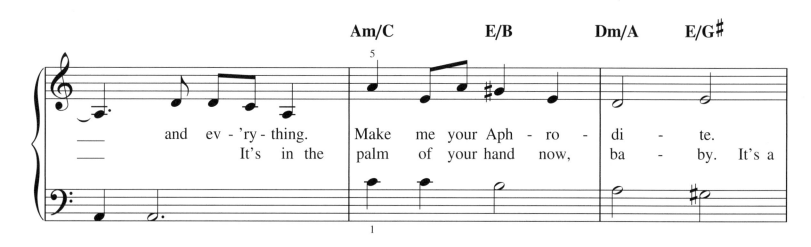

**Am/C**  **E/B**  **Dm/A**  **E/G♯**

_____ and ev - 'ry - thing. Make me your Aph - ro - di - te.
_____ It's in the palm of your hand now, ba - by. It's a

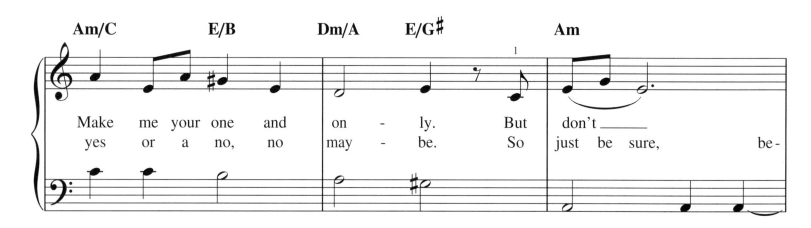

**Am/C**  **E/B**  **Dm/A**  **E/G♯**  **Am**

Make me your one and on - ly. But don't _____
yes or a no, no may - be. So just be sure, be-

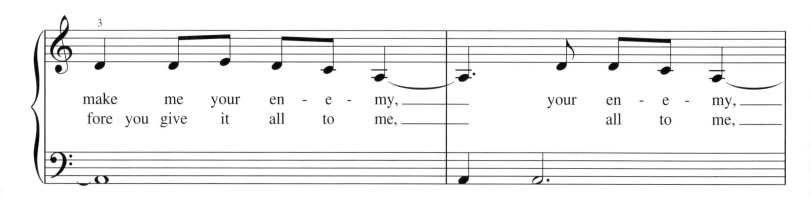

make me your en - e - my, _____ your en - e - my, _____
fore you give it all to me, _____ all to me,

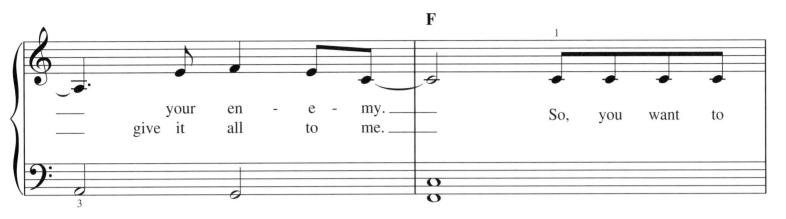

your en - e - my. ___
give it all to me. ___

F

So, you want to

C

play with mag - ic,

Am

boy, you should know

G

what you're fall - ing for. ___

F

Ba - by, do you

C

dare to do ___ this?

Am

'Cause I'm com - ing

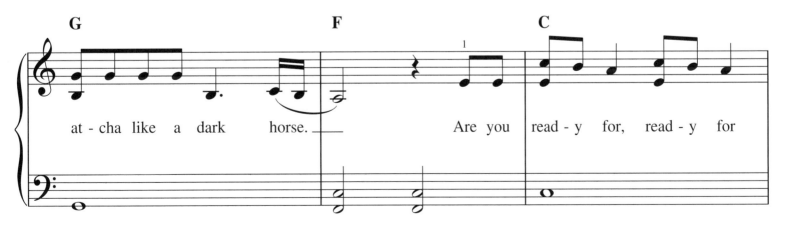

G

at - cha like a dark horse. ___

F

Are you read - y for, read - y for

C

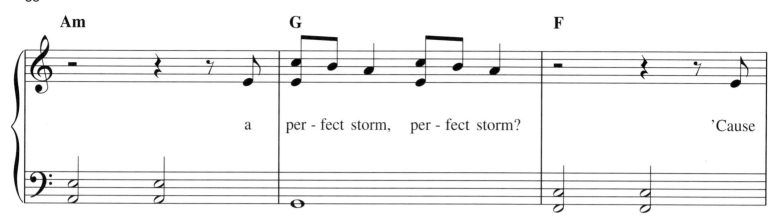

a  per - fect storm,  per - fect storm?  'Cause

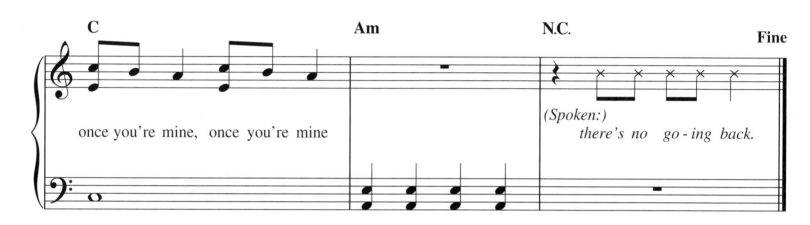

once you're mine, once you're mine

(Spoken:)
there's no  go - ing  back.

(See rap lyrics)

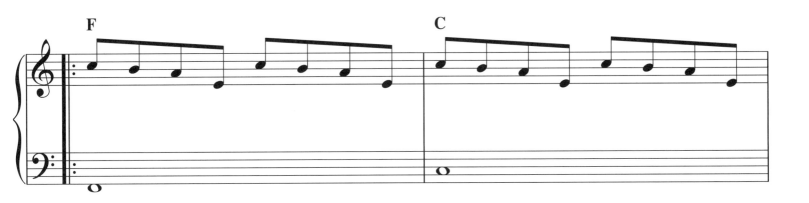

*Rap lyrics*

She's a beast
I call her Karma
She'll eat your heart out
Like Jeffrey Dahmer

Be careful
Try not to lead her on
Shorty heart is on steroids
'Cause her love is so strong

You may fall in love when you meet her
If you get the chance, you better keep her
She's sweet as pie, but if you break her heart
She'll turn cold as a freezer

That fairy tale ending with a knight in shining armor
She can be my Sleeping Beauty
I'm gon' put her in a coma

Now I think I love her
Shorty so bad, sprung and I don't care
She ride me like a roller coaster
Turned the bedroom into a fair

Her love is like a drug
I was tryna hit it and quit it
But lil' mama so dope
I messed around and got addicted

# THIS IS HOW WE DO

Words and Music by KATY PERRY,
KLAS AHLUND and MAX MARTIN

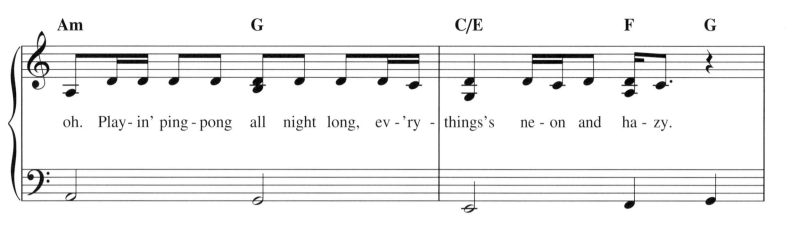

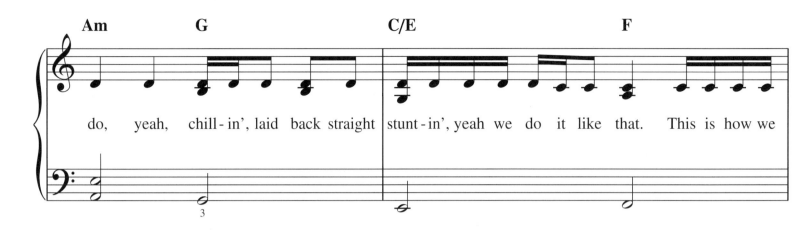

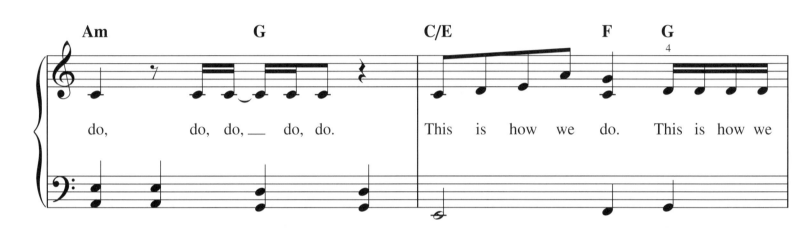

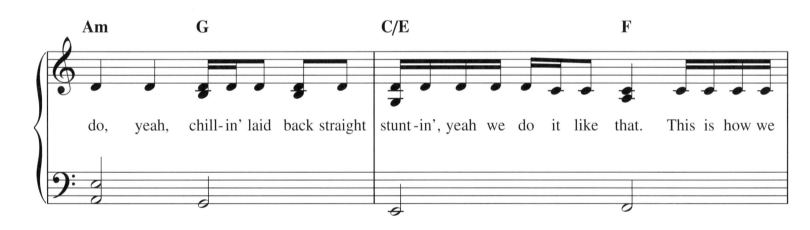

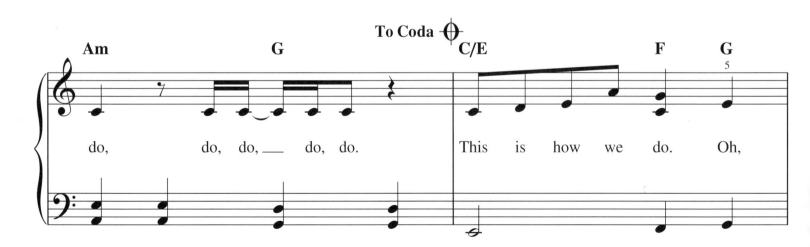

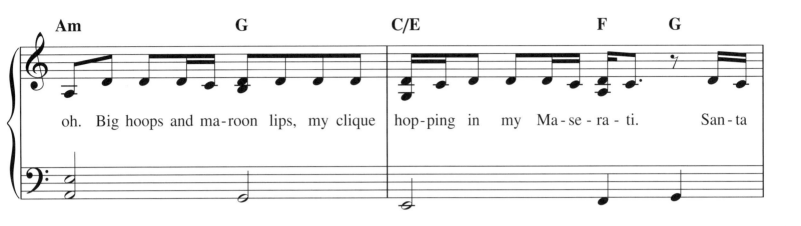

oh. Big hoops and ma-roon lips, my clique | hop-ping in my Ma-se-ra-ti. San-ta

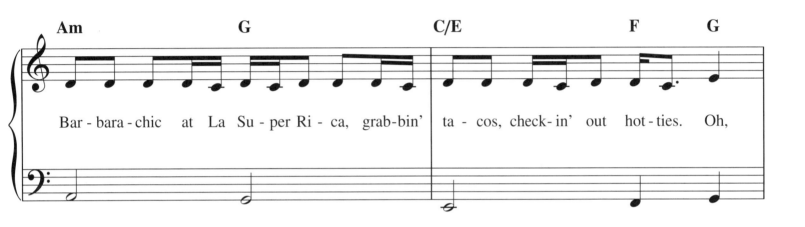

Bar-bara-chic at La Su-per Ri-ca, grab-bin' | ta-cos, check-in' out hot-ties. Oh,

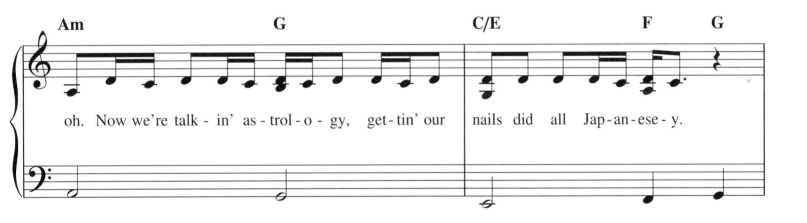

oh. Now we're talk-in' as-trol-o-gy, get-tin' our | nails did all Jap-an-ese-y.

**D.S. al Coda**

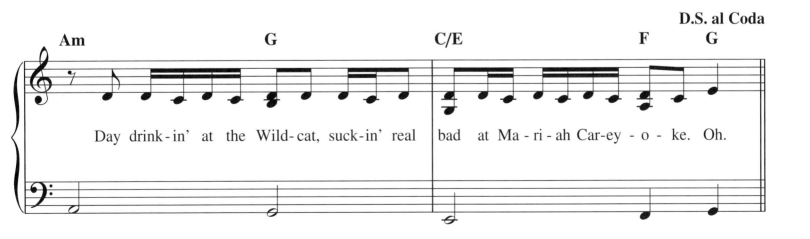

Day drink-in' at the Wild-cat, suck-in' real | bad at Ma-ri-ah Car-ey-o-ke. Oh.

**CODA**

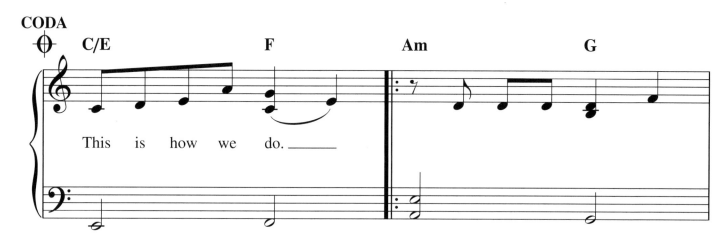

This is how we do. _____

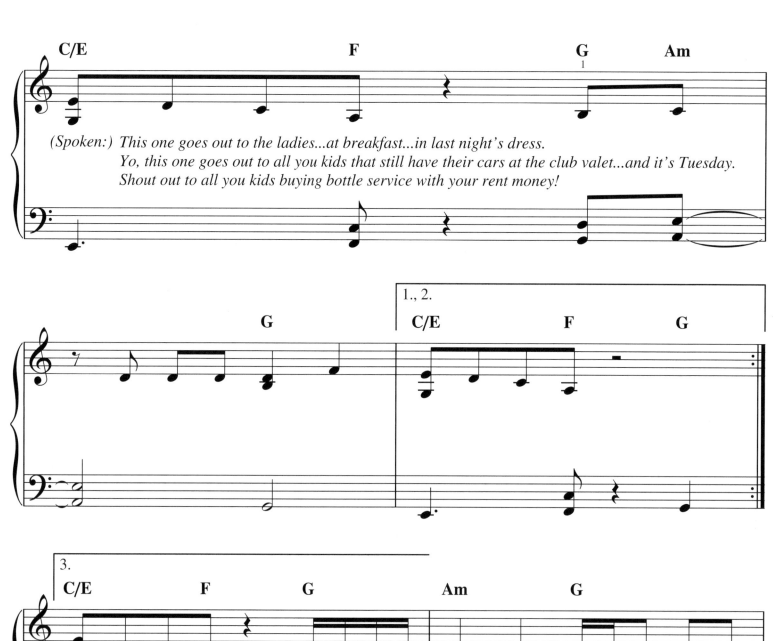

*(Spoken:)* *This one goes out to the ladies...at breakfast...in last night's dress.*
*Yo, this one goes out to all you kids that still have their cars at the club valet...and it's Tuesday.*
*Shout out to all you kids buying bottle service with your rent money!*

1., 2.

3.

*Re-spect!*          *(Sung:)* This is how we      do,      yeah,      chill-in' laid  back straight

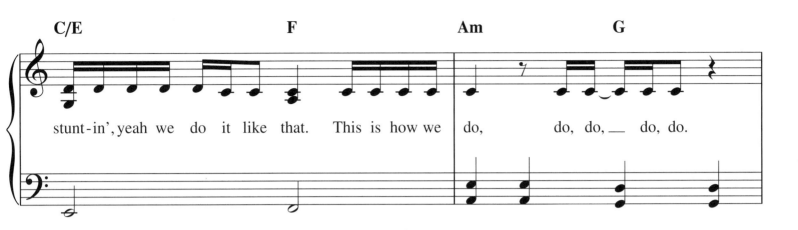

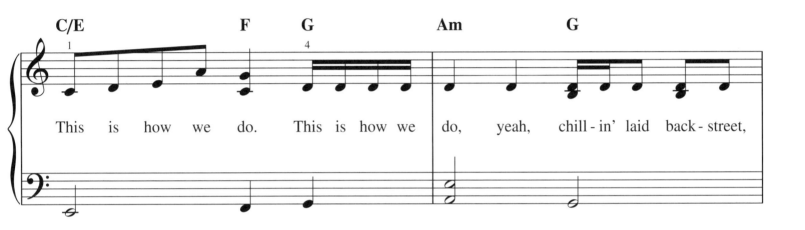

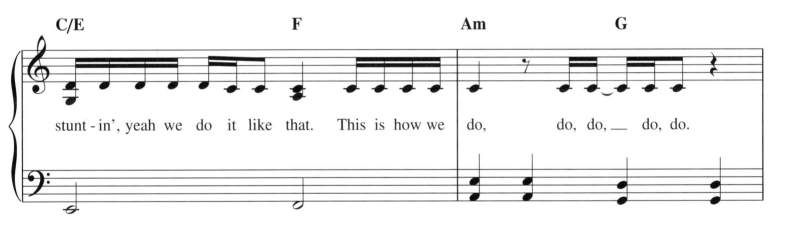

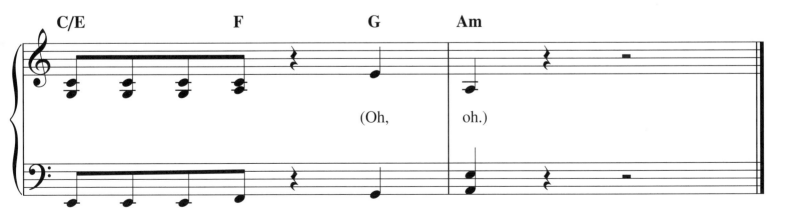

# INTERNATIONAL SMILE

Words and Music by KATY PERRY,
LUKASZ GOTTWALD, MAX MARTIN
and HENRY WALTER

Flow - ers in her hair, she don't care.
*She's got that "Je ne sais quoi," you know it.*

Peach pink lips, yeah, ev-'ry-bod-y stares.
*So trés chic, yeah, she's a clas - sic.*

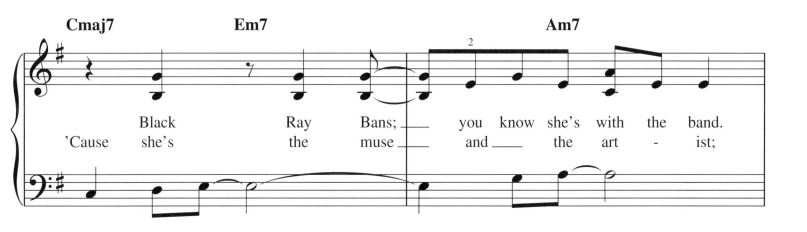

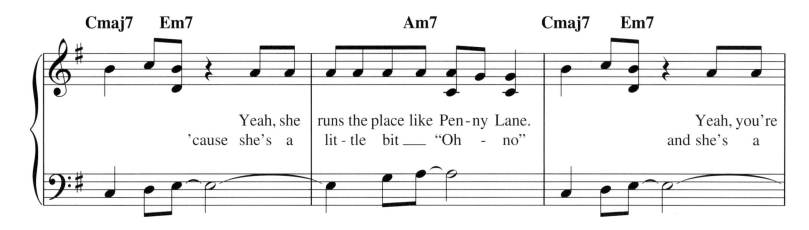

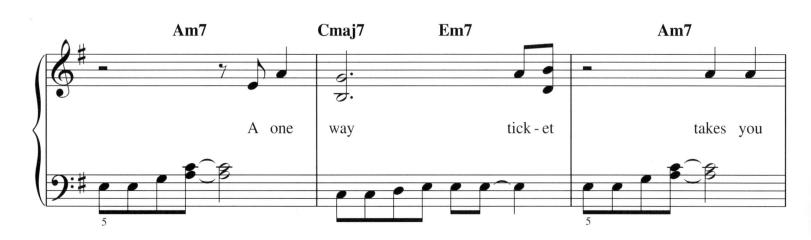

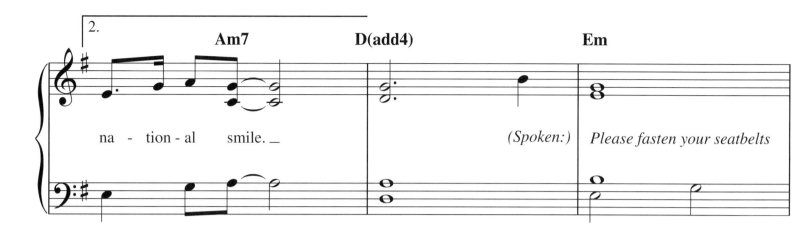

na - tion - al smile. _

*(Spoken:)* *Please fasten your seatbelts*

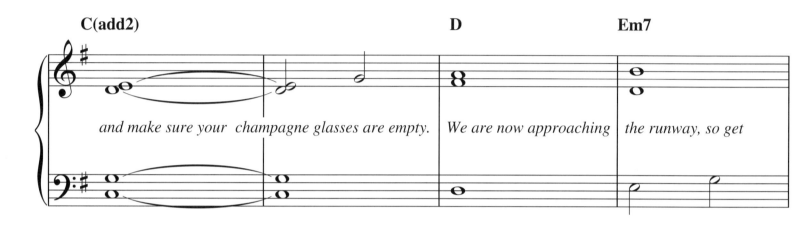

*and make sure your champagne glasses are empty.* *We are now approaching* *the runway, so get*

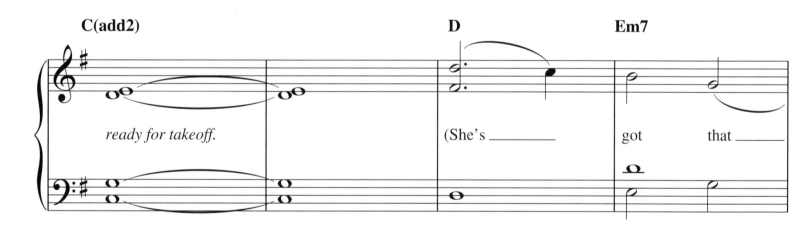

*ready for takeoff.* (She's _____ got that _____

_____ in - ter - na - tion - al

# GHOST

Words and Music by KATY PERRY,
LUKASZ GOTTWALD, MAX MARTIN,
BONNIE McKEE and HENRY WALTER

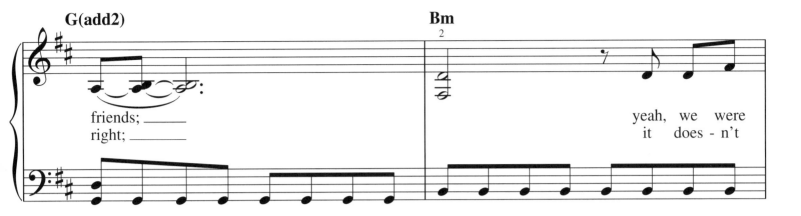

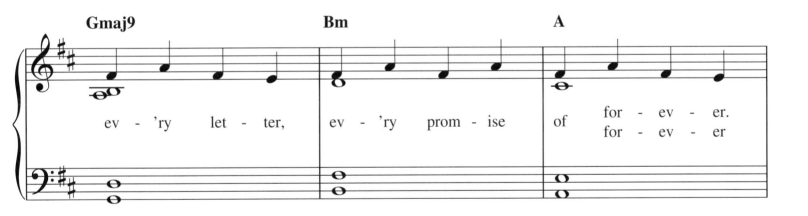

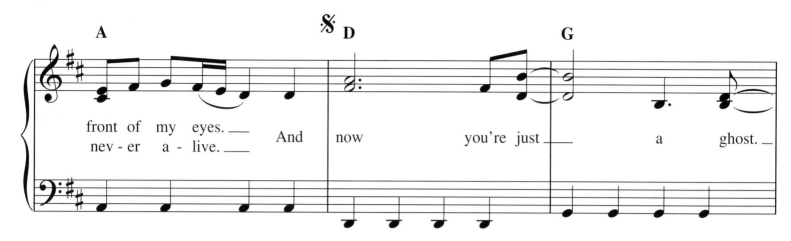

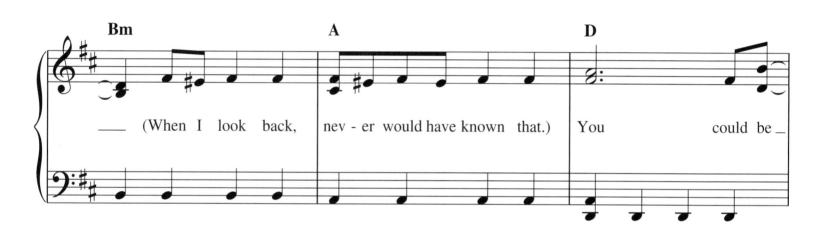

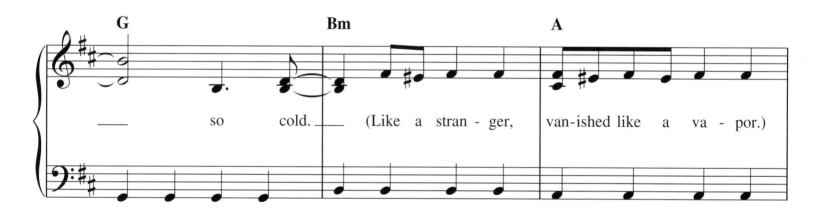

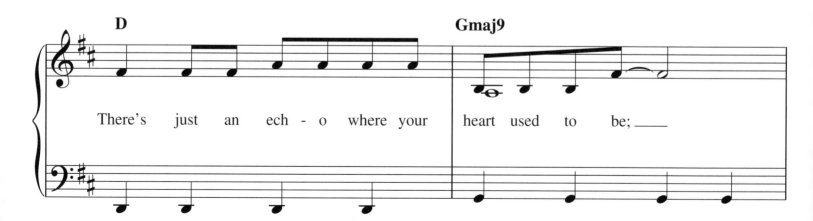

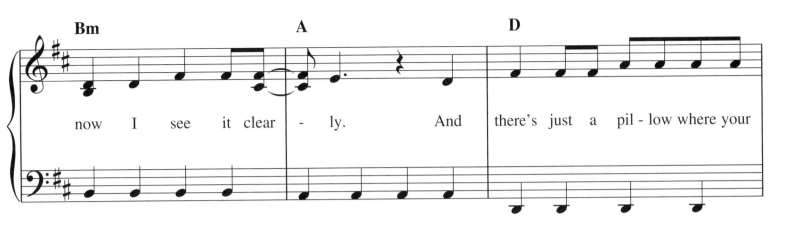

now I see it clear - ly. And there's just a pil - low where your

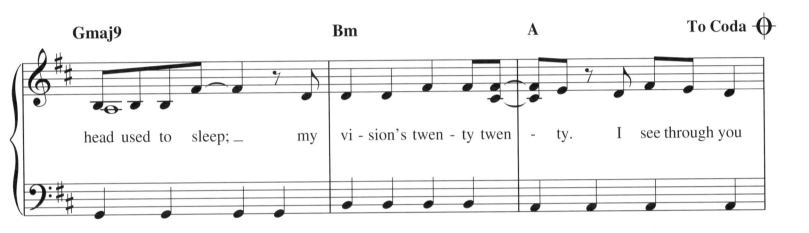

**To Coda**

head used to sleep; — my vi - sion's twen - ty twen - ty. I see through you

1.

now. Some-thing has

2.

now, now, now, now, now,

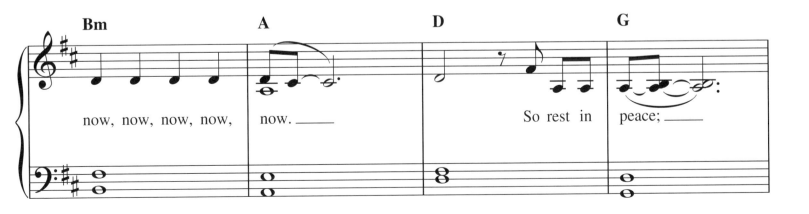

now, now, now, now, now. _____ So rest in peace; _____

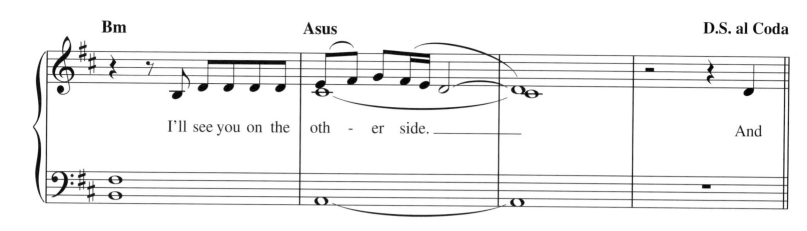

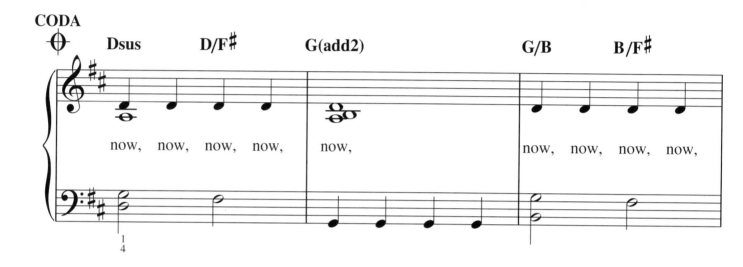

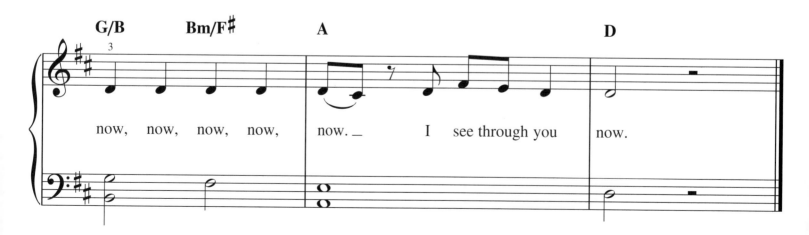

# LOVE ME

Words and Music by KATY PERRY,
MAX MARTIN, CHRISTIAN "BLOODSHY" KARLSSON,
VINCENT PONTARE and MANGUS LIDEHALL

**Moderately fast**

*With pedal*

I lost my- self ___ in fear ___ of
times I ___ wish ___ my skin ___ was

los- ing ___ you. ___ I wish I ___ did- n't ___
a cos- tume ___ that I could ___ just ___

___ do, but I did. ___ I
un- zip and ___ strip. ___ But

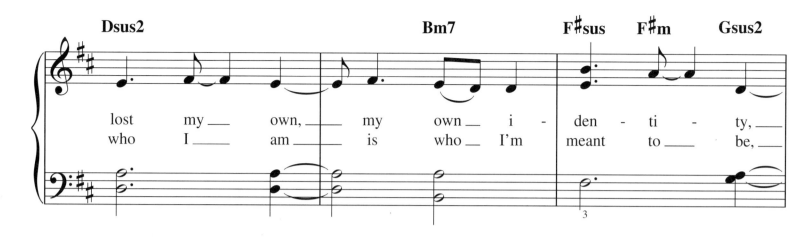

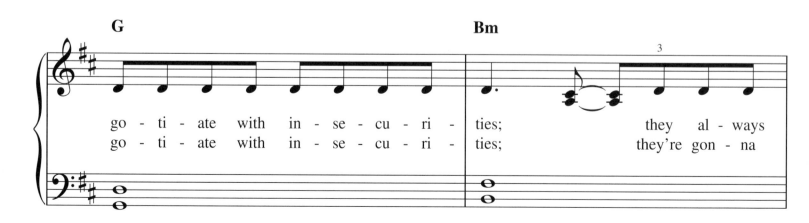

seem to get the best of ___ me. ___
have to take a back ___ seat. ___
I found I
I know I

**G**                 **Bsus**    **Bm**

had to love my - self the way I want you ___ to ___
have to love my - self the way I want you ___ to ___

          **Dsus2**      **D**              **Bm7**

___ love me.
___ love me. No more sec - ond guess - ing; ___

**F#sus**   **F#m**         **G**             **D**

___ no, there's no more ques - tion - ing. ___ I'll be the

one de - fin - ing who I'm ___ gon - na be. ___

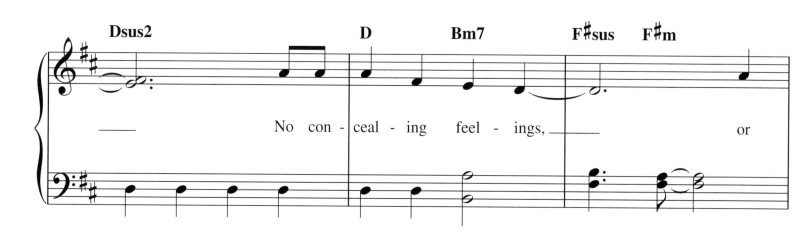

___ No con - ceal - ing feel - ings, ___ or

chang - ing sea - son - 'ly. ___ I'm gon - na love my - self the way I

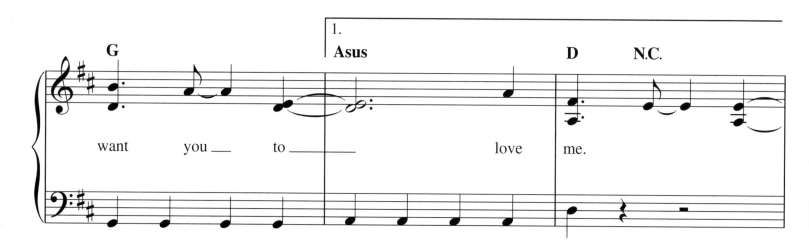

want you ___ to ___ love me.

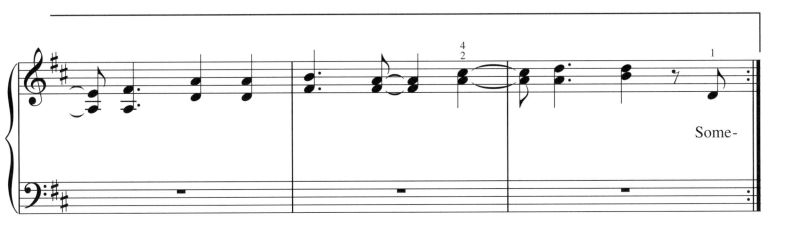

Some-

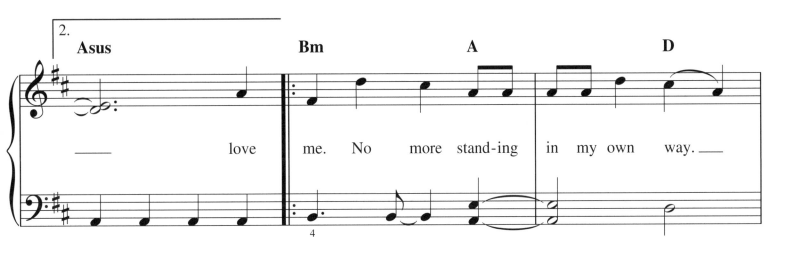

love me. No more stand-ing in my own way.

Let's go deep-er, Let's get clos-er. No more stand-ing

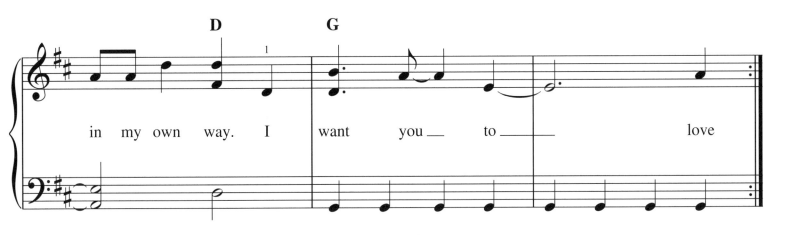

in my own way. I want you to love

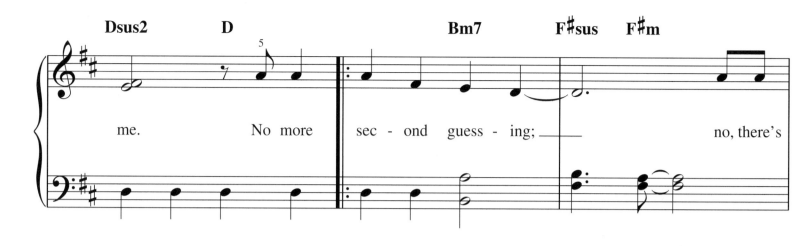

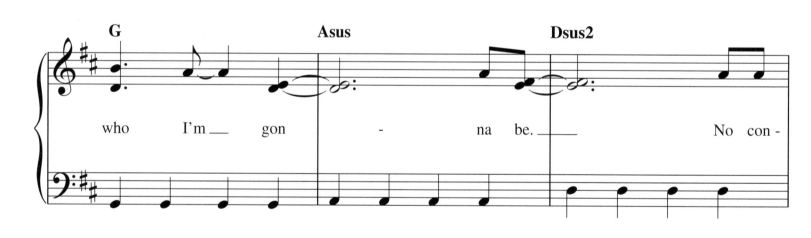

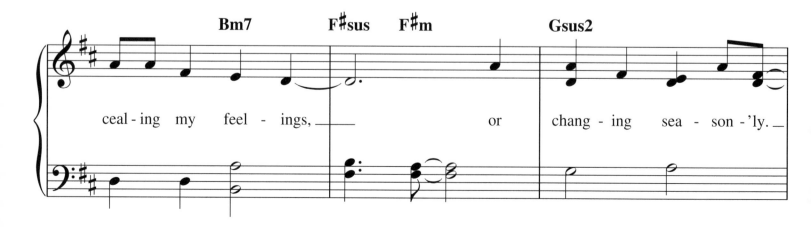

# THIS MOMENT

Words and Music by KATY PERRY,
TOR HERMANSEN, MIKKEL ERIKSEN
and BENJAMIN LEVIN

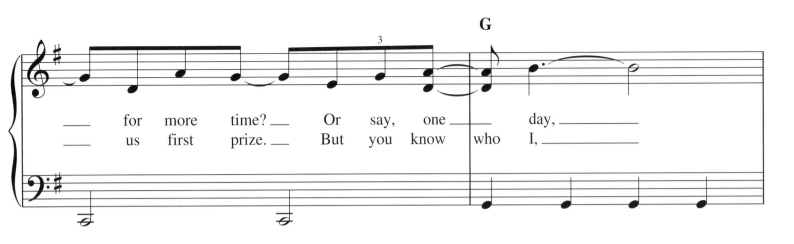

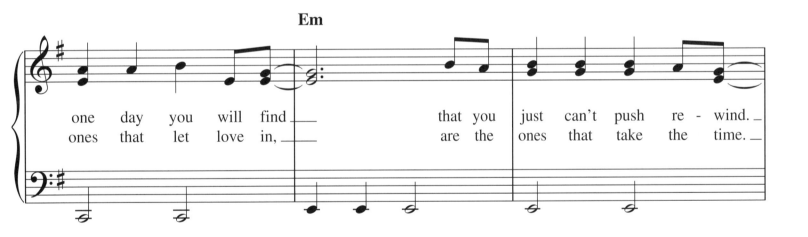

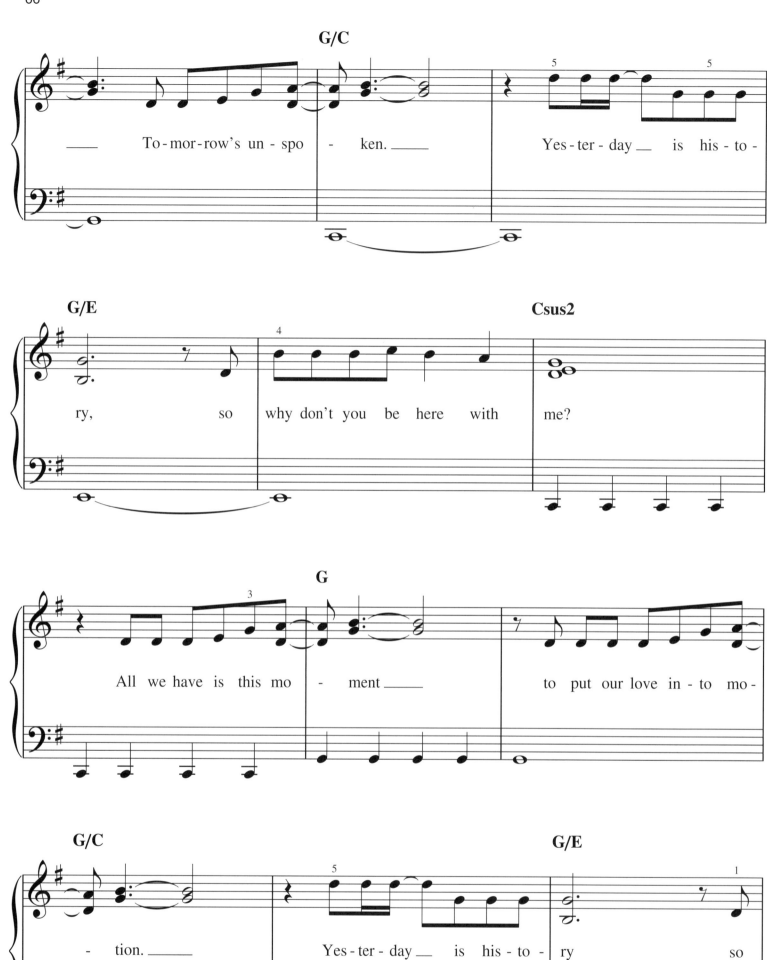

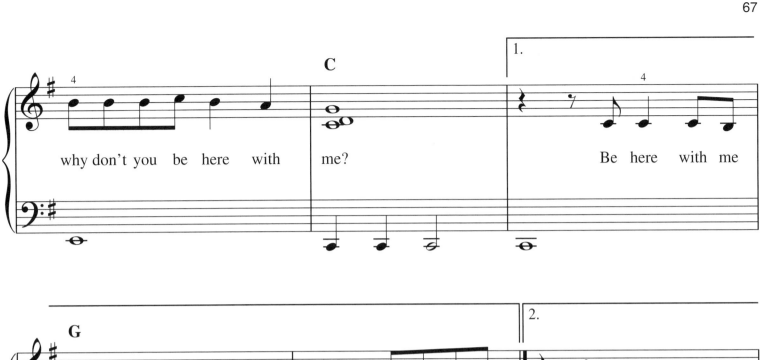

why don't you be here with me? Be here with me

now. Do you ev - er Be here with me

now. Be here with me now.

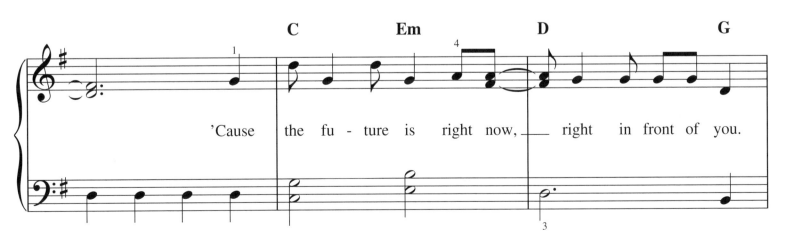

'Cause the fu - ture is right now, right in front of you.

# DOUBLE RAINBOW

Words and Music by KATY PERRY,
SIA FURLER and GREGORY KURSTIN

**Moderate Pop**

You're a one of a one, __
Se - cret-ly, __ hit the

a one of a kind __ once in a
lot - ter - y __ 'cause you're that you on - ly find __ bright - er than __ all of the

life - time. Made to fit __ like a
north - ern lights. You speak to me __ e - ven

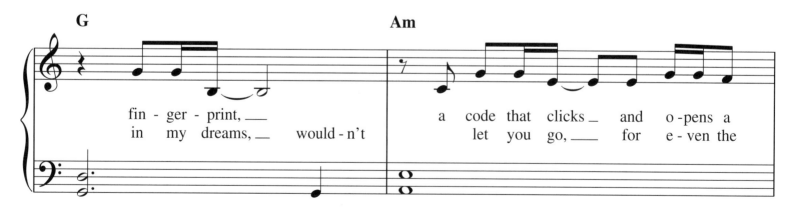

fin - ger - print, __ a code that clicks __ and o - pens a
in my dreams, __ would-n't let you go, __ for e - ven the

- bow in the sky. And wher - ev - er you go, so will I.

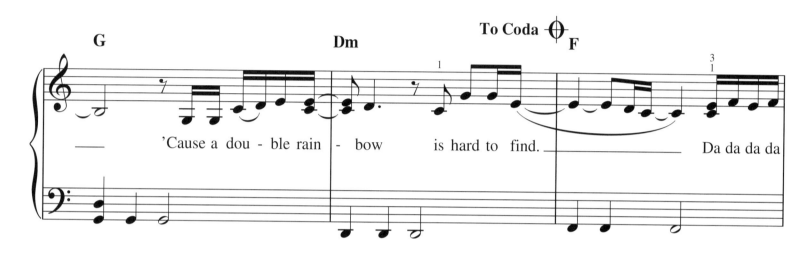

'Cause a dou - ble rain - bow is hard to find. Da da da da

da, da da da da da. Was a phe - nom - e - non when you

came a - long. Yeah, our chem - is - try was more than sci - ence. It was

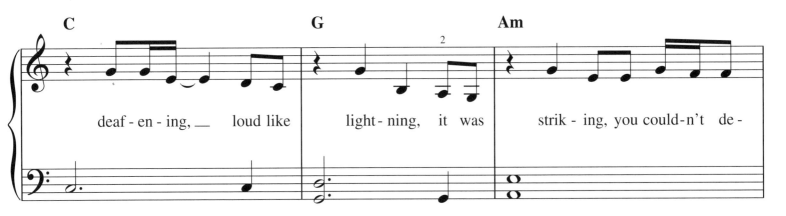

**C**　　　　　　　**G**　　　　　　**Am**

deaf - en - ing, __ loud like　light - ning, it was　strik - ing, you could-n't de -

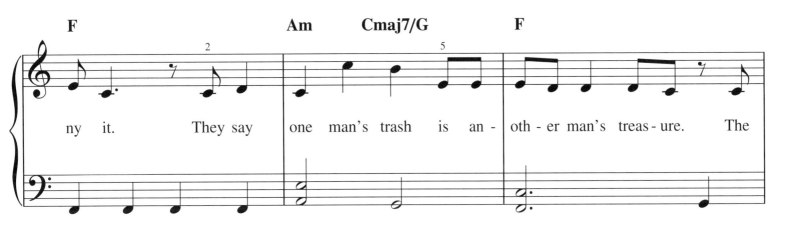

**F**　　　　　　**Am**　**Cmaj7/G**　　**F**

ny it. They say　one man's trash is an - oth - er man's treas - ure. The

**A**　　**Cmaj7/G**　　**F**　　　　　　　　**D.S. al Coda**

two of us to-geth-er make　ev-'ry-thing　glit - ter. __　'Cause I un-der - stand __

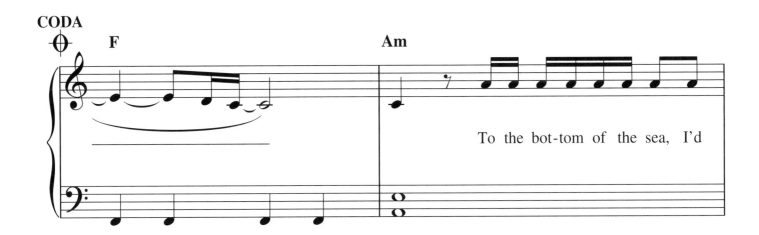

**CODA**　**F**　　　　　　　　　　**Am**

To the bot-tom of the sea, I'd

go to find _ you. Climb the high-est peak to be right be-side _ you.

Ev-'ry step I take, _____ I'm keep-ing you in mind. _____

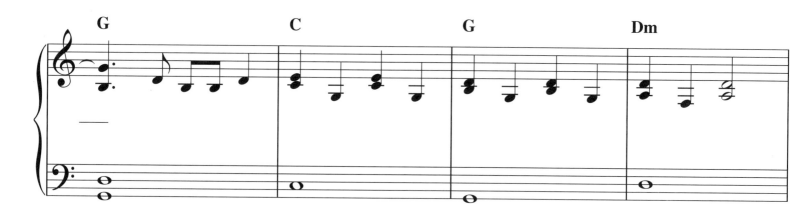

Ooh _ ooh. _ 'Cause I un-der-stand _____ you, we see eye to eye _

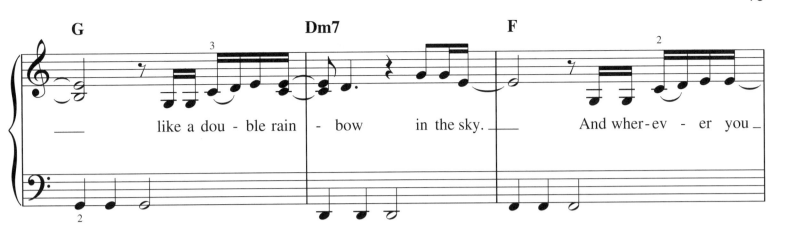

like a dou - ble rain - bow in the sky. ___ And wher-ev - er you ___

___ go, so will I. ___ 'Cause a dou - ble rain - bow is hard to find. ___

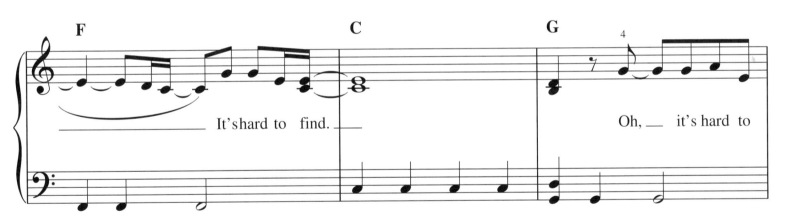

It's hard to find. ___ Oh, ___ it's hard to

find. Once in a life - time.

# BY THE GRACE OF GOD

Words and Music by KATY PERRY
and GREG WELLS

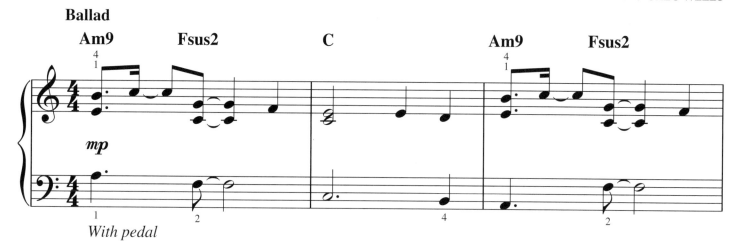

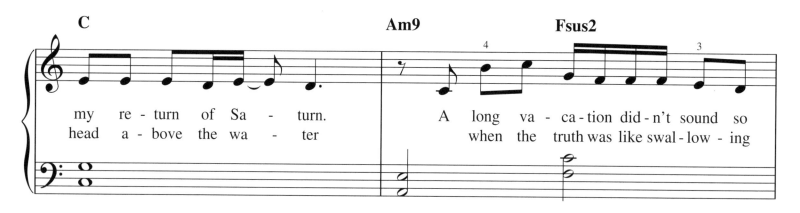

Was twen-ty sev - en, sur - viv - ing ___
I thank my sis - ter for keep - ing my

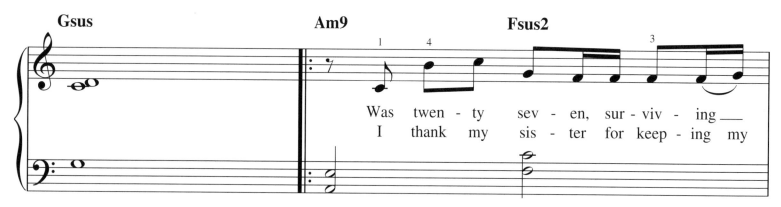

my re-turn of Sa - turn.
head a - bove the wa - ter

A long va - ca-tion did-n't sound so
when the truth was like swal-low-ing

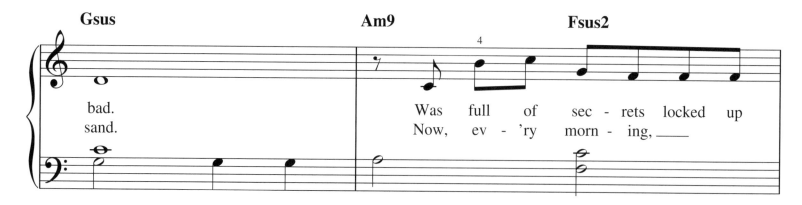

bad.
sand.

Was full of sec - rets locked up
Now, ev - 'ry morn - ing, ___

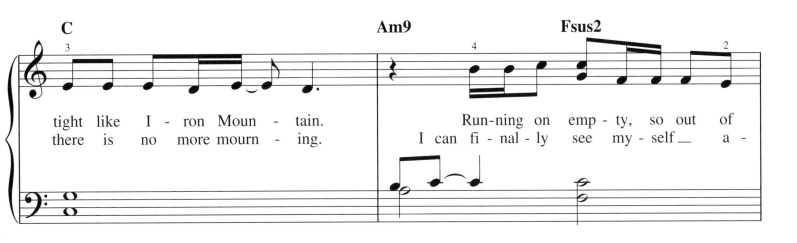

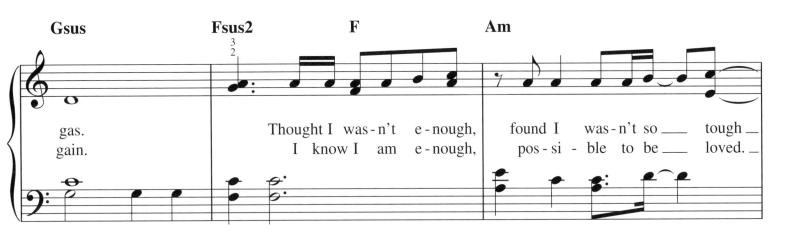

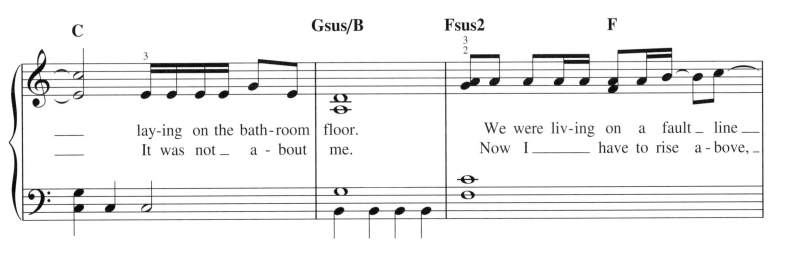

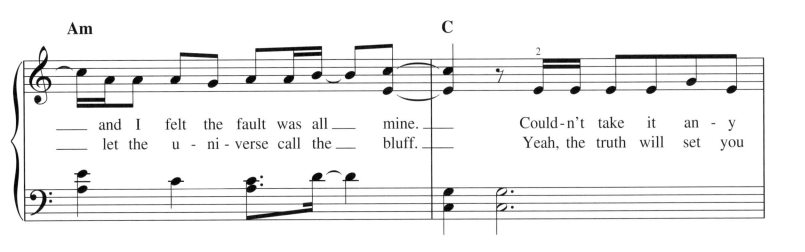

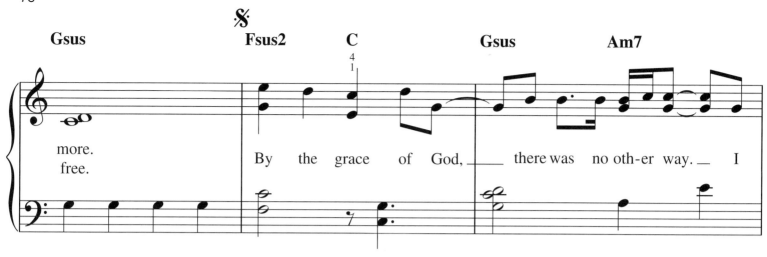

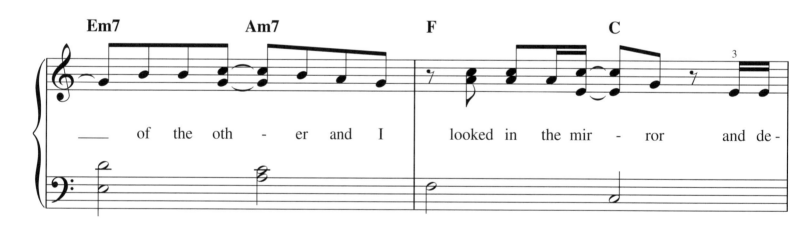

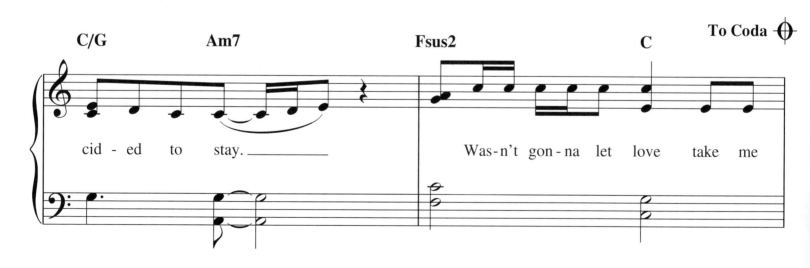

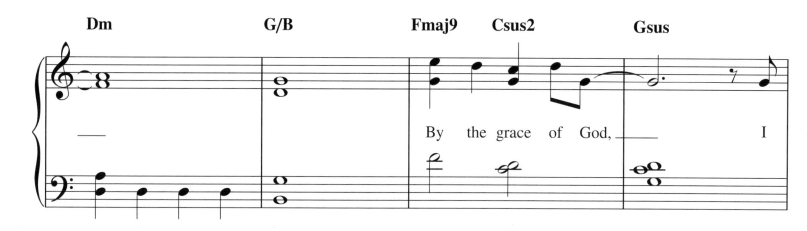

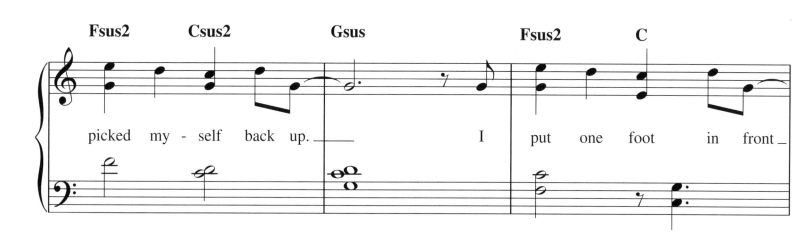

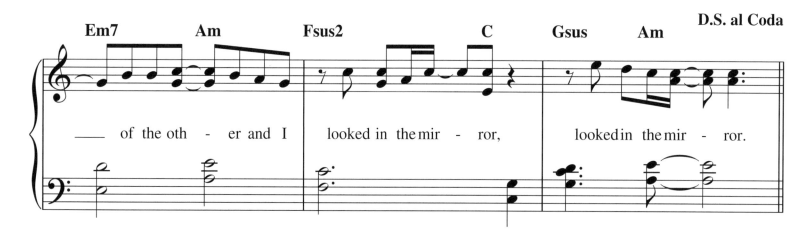

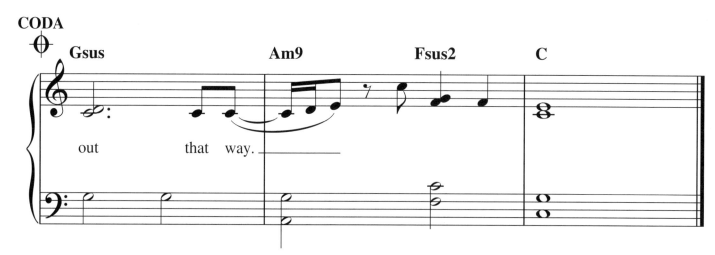

# SPIRITUAL

Words and Music by KATY PERRY,
GREGORY KURSTIN and JOHN MAYER

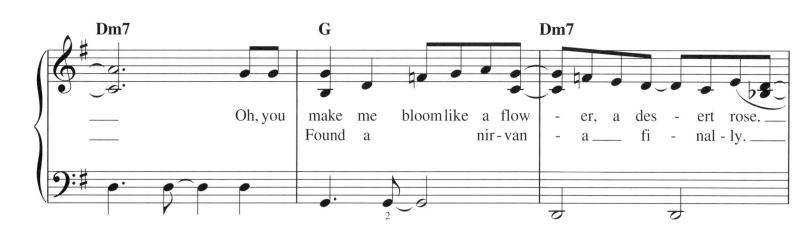

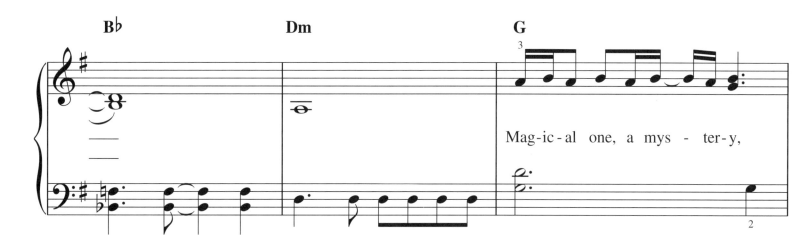

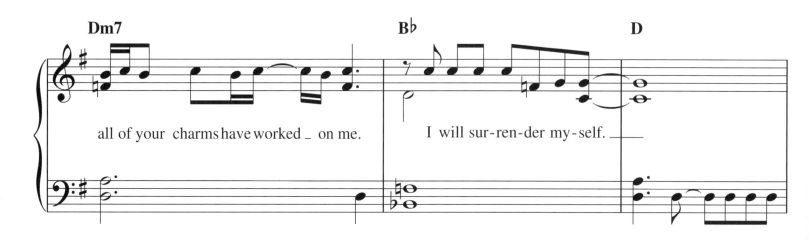

Ho-ly hell __ and heav-en high, __ you have o - pened up my eyes, __ and I am fi-nal-ly healed. __

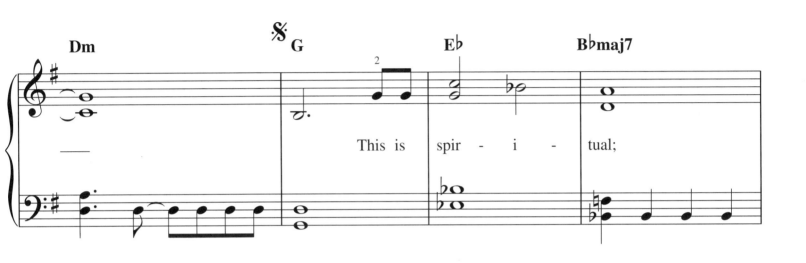

This is spir - i - tual;

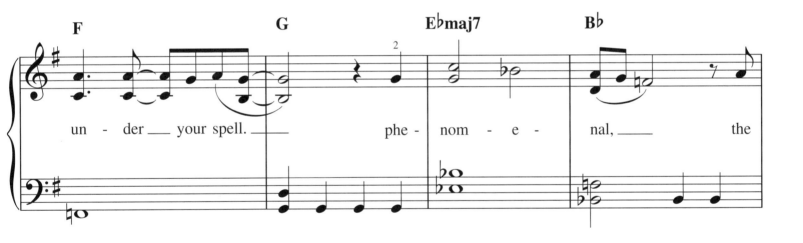

un - der __ your spell. __ phe - nom - e - nal, __ the

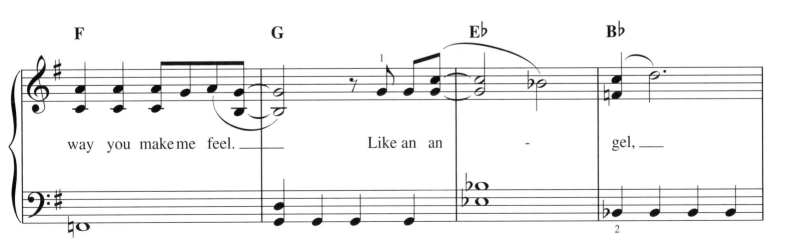

way you make me feel. __ Like an an - gel, __

all    a - glow.     Like   a   feath -

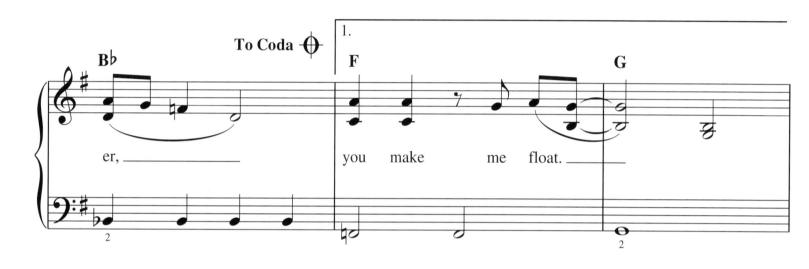

er,         you   make    me   float.

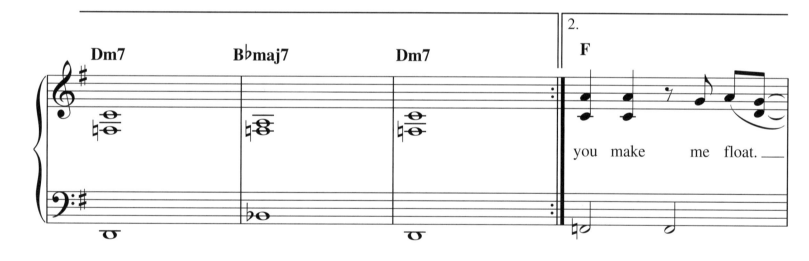

you   make    me   float.

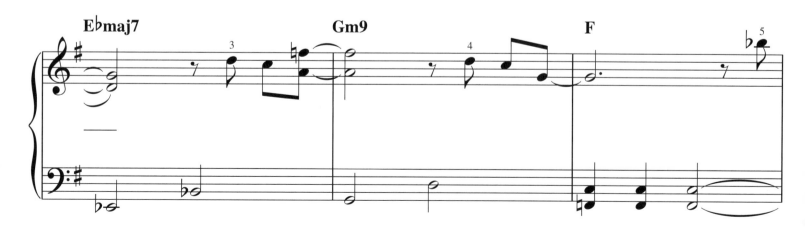

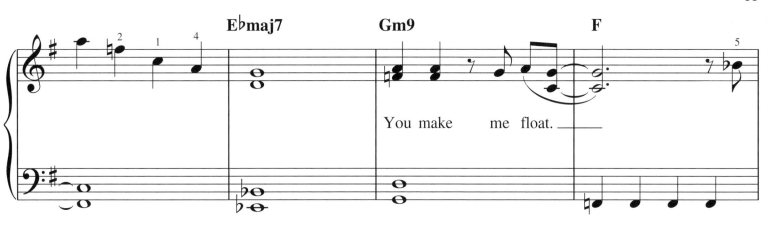

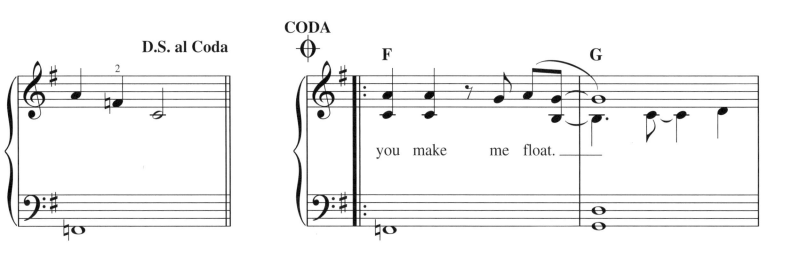

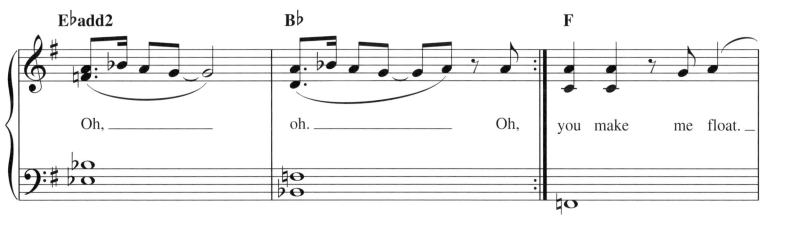

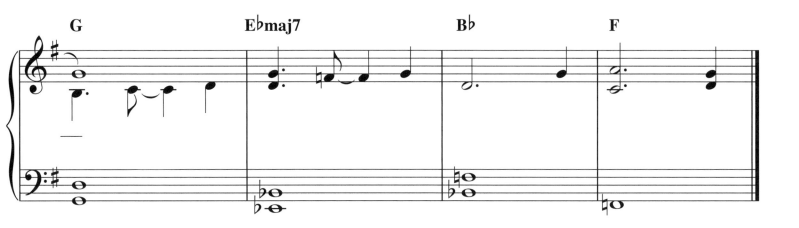

# IT TAKES TWO

Words and Music by KATY PERRY,
TOR HERMANSEN, MIKKEL ERIKSEN,
BENJAMIN LEVIN and EMELI SANDE

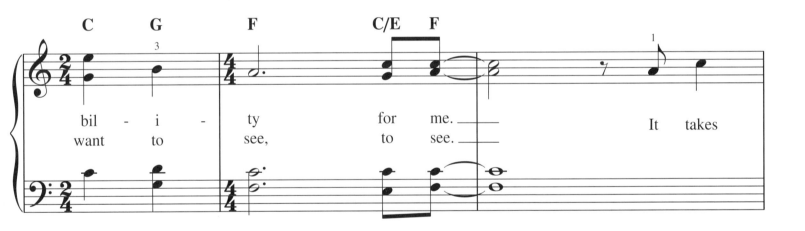

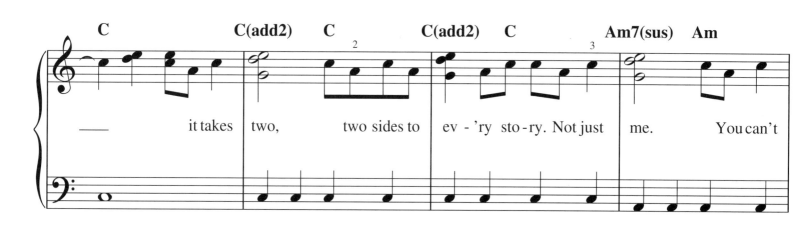

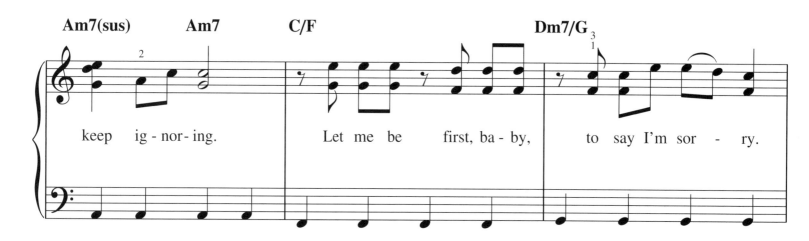

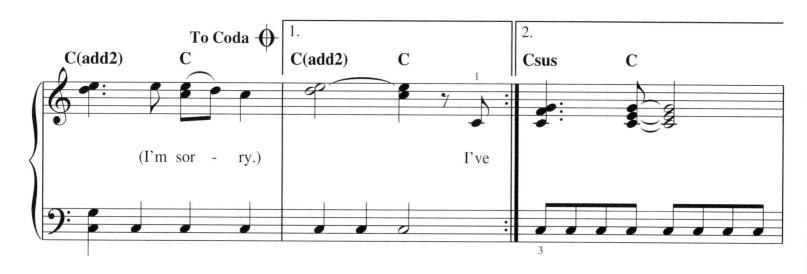

# CHOOSE YOUR BATTLES

Words and Music by KATY PERRY,
JONATHA BROOKE and GREG WELLS

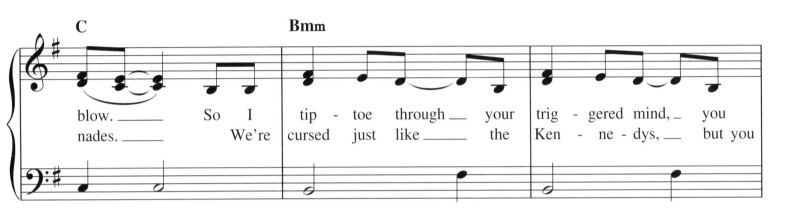

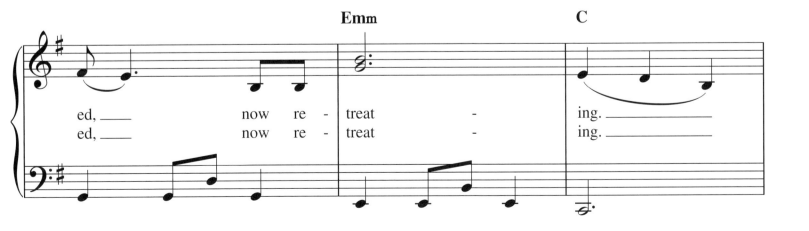

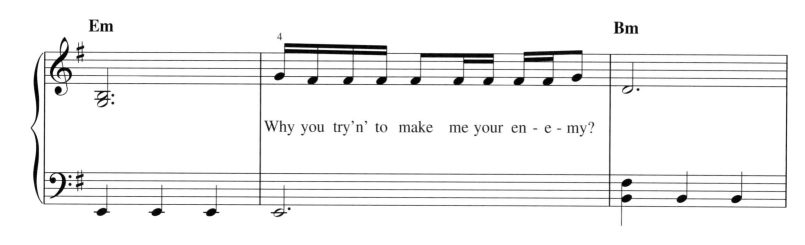

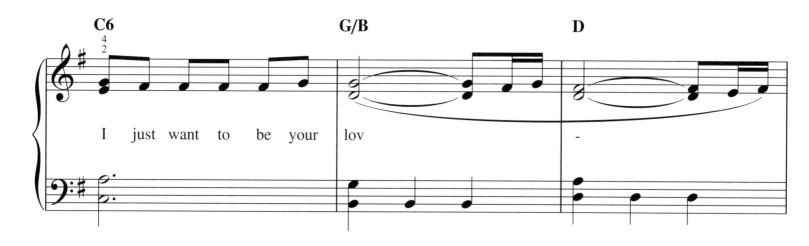

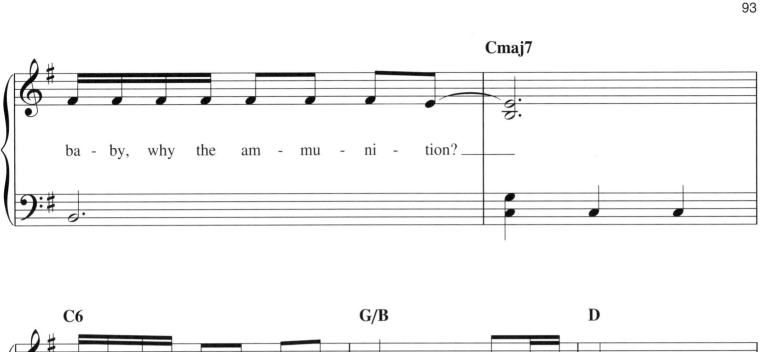

baby, why the am - mu - ni - tion? _____

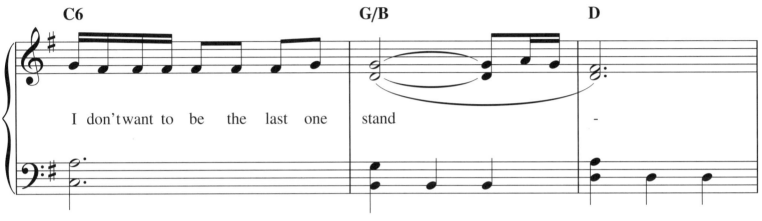

I don't want to be the last one stand -

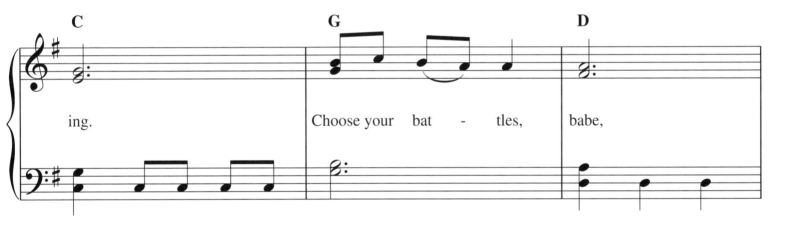

ing. Choose your bat - tles, babe,

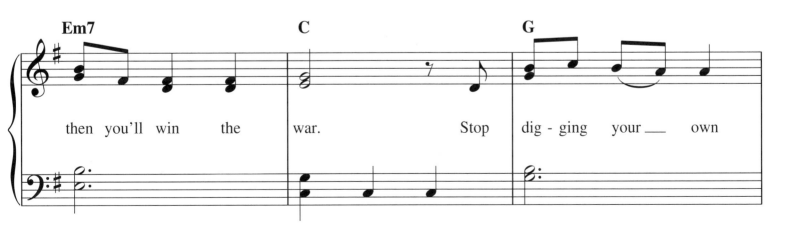

then you'll win the war. Stop dig - ging your ___ own

grave when there's _ so much to live _____ for.

Choose your bat - tles, babe, 'cause I'm not fight - ing an - y -

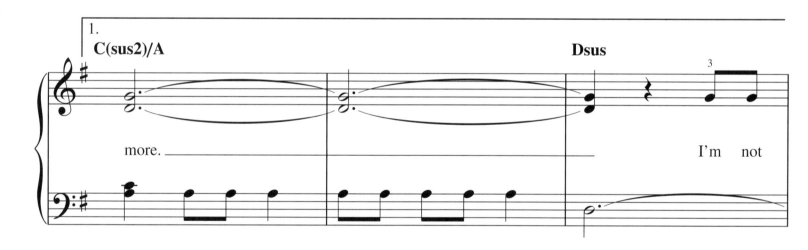

more. _____ I'm not

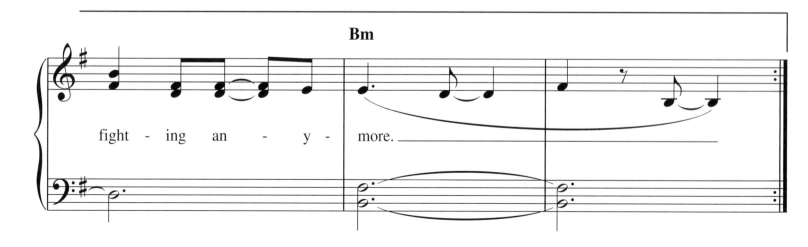

fight - ing an - y - more. _____

more.     No, _____   I'm not

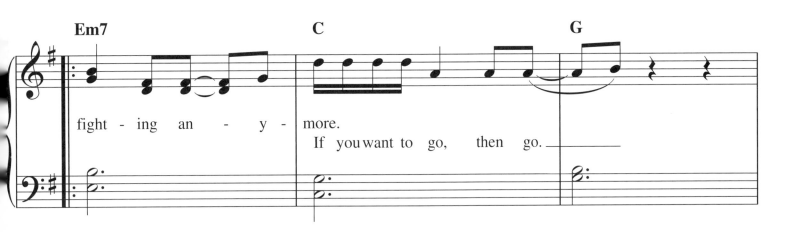

fight - ing an - y - more.

If you want to go,  then go. _____

If you want to stay,  then stay. _____  'Cause I don't want to fight no more, ___

_____  ba - by. ___  I'm not fight - ing an - y - more.